Awesome Yo-Yo *Tricks*

STERLING INNOVATION
An imprint of Sterling Publishing Co., Inc.

New York / London
www.sterlingpublishing.com

10 9 8 7 6 5 4 3 2

Published in 2009 by Sterling Publishing Co., Inc.
387 Park Avenue South, New York, NY 10016

Distributed in Canada by Sterling Publishing
c/o Canadian Manda Group, 165 Dufferin Street
Toronto, Ontario, Canada M6K 3H6
Distributed in the United Kingdom by GMC Distribution Services
Castle Place, 166 High Street, Lewes, East Sussex, England BN7 1XU
Distributed in Australia by Capricorn Link (Australia) Pty. Ltd.
P.O. Box 704, Windsor, NSW 2756, Australia

Cover design by Gary Martin

Printed in China

Sterling ISBN 978-1-4027-6917-7

For information about custom editions, special sales, premium and corporate purchases, please contact Sterling Special Sales Department at 800-805-5489 or specialsales@sterlingpublishing.com.

Contents

Introduction

This book is designed for the beginner. Once you have mastered your throws, you can move on to more difficult maneuvers. The tricks are classified within each section: a trick with one yo-yo ( ) is the simplest. Two yo-yos are intermediate. Three are advanced, and four are for experts only.

Now, grab your favorite yo-yo and get started!

Who is this tiny person and what is she doing here? **See page 40 for an explanation.**

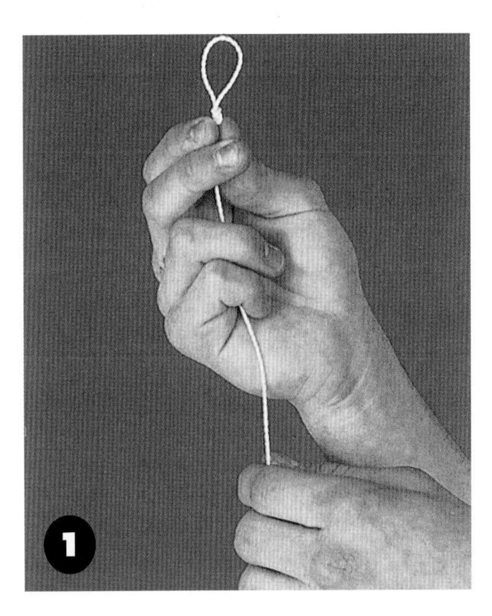

Yo-Yo Basics

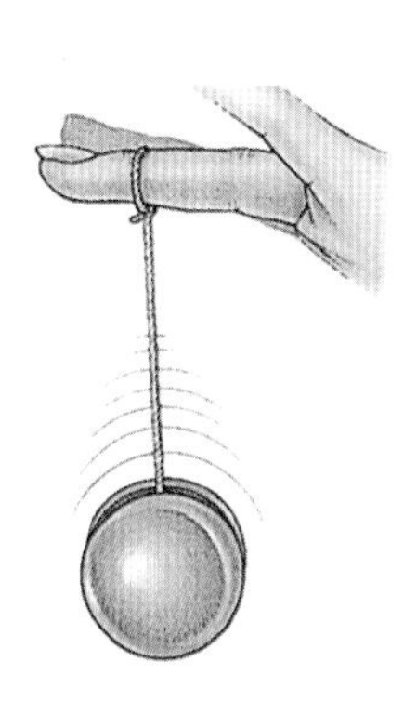

How to Put a Yo-Yo on Your Finger

Thanks to yo-yo string manufacturers, you can easily tell which end of the string is which. The part with the tied loop is the top and the other end is the bottom that fits around the axle. DO NOT put your finger through the loop! Instead, run part of the string back through the loop to create a “slip knot.” Place your middle finger through this slip knot and tighten it so it won’t slide off. The string should be about halfway between your first and second knuckle.

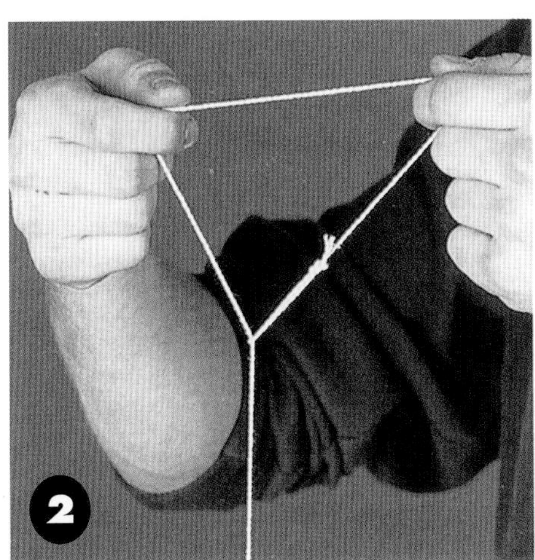

How Long Should My String Be?

Place your finger in the slip knot loop and let the yo-yo fall to the floor. Hold your hand even with your navel. If your string is the correct length, it should just graze the floor. Unless you are over five feet tall, chances are you will need to trim the string. With the yo-yo on the floor, measure the string 3 inches (7.5 cm) above your navel and cut the string. Tie a knotted loop, just like the one you just cut off, then run a slip knot back through the string.

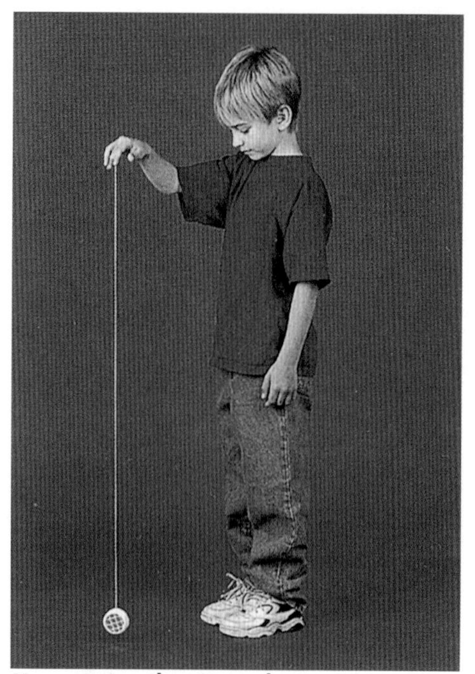

Yo-yo string that is too long

Now What?

Wind the string back into the yo-yo. For looser tension, wind the string toward you. For more tension, wind the yo-yo away from you.

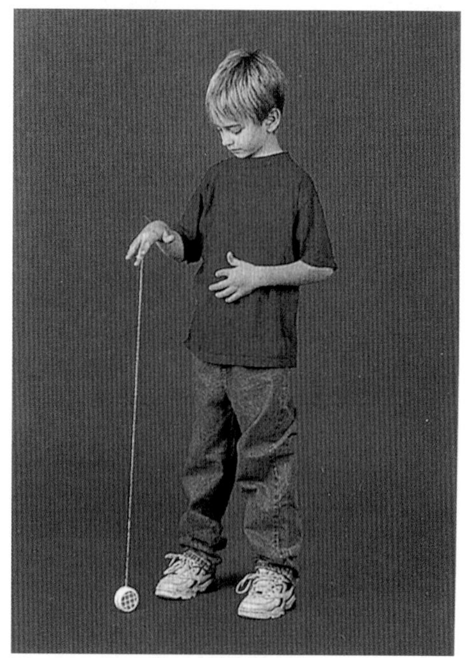

Yo-yo string the right length

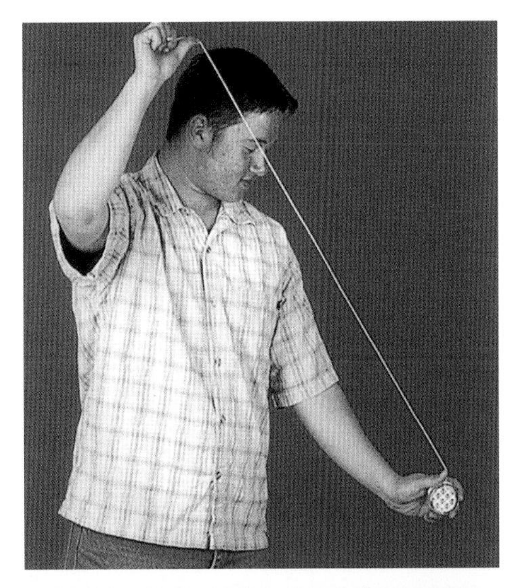

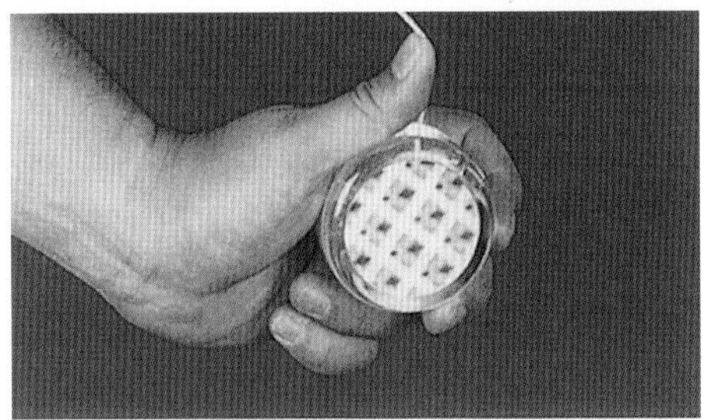

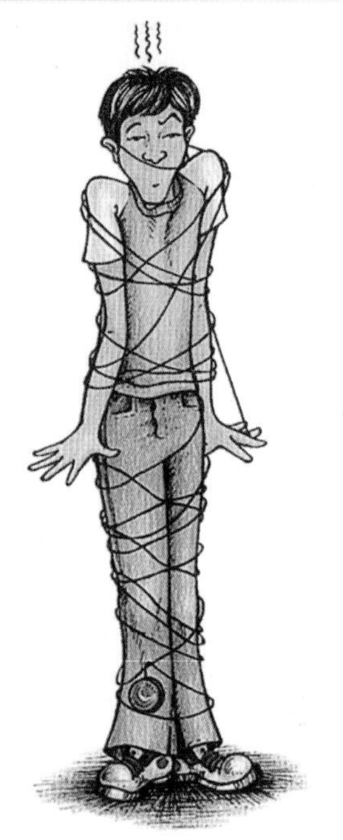

Thumb Wind

One way of getting a string around a yo-yo is called a thumb wind.

1. Place your yo-yo hand up above your shoulder, about even with the top of your head.

2. Place the thumb of your free hand in the space between the two sides of your yo-yo. Your thumb should be pressing forward into the string. Hold the bottom end of the yo-yo with your pointer finger.

3. Pull the string taut between your two hands.

4. To get it to wind back up, push down with your thumb and lift with your yo-yo hand at the same time. The yo-yo will not come all the way up, but you can dribble it up to your hand using several up-and-down motions.

Plan B

1. Another variation of the thumb wind is to use two fingers wrapped around the string. Use your fingers to spin the yo-yo out, pushing downward while pulling the string up.

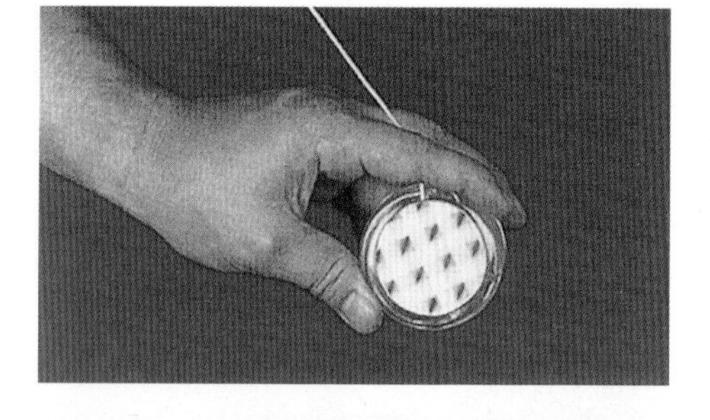

If All Else Fails

Hold the yo-yo in your free hand. Leave plenty of slack and wind the string up around the yo-yo.

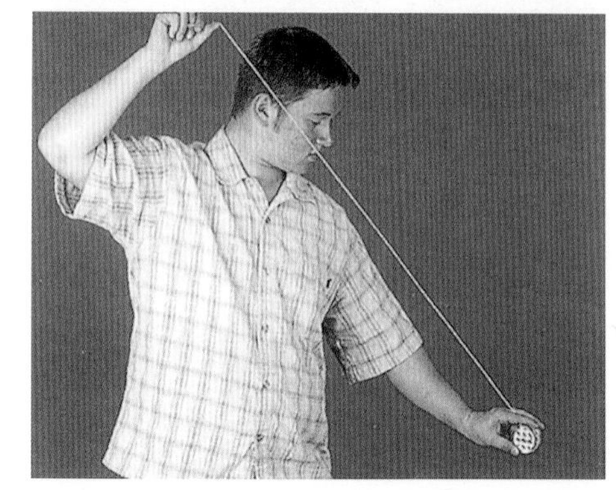

Holding a Yo-Yo

This is probably intuitive, but just in case it's not, here goes: Put the string on your finger. Cup the yo-yo in the palm of your hand so that the string winds around the top of the yo-yo and goes toward your finger.

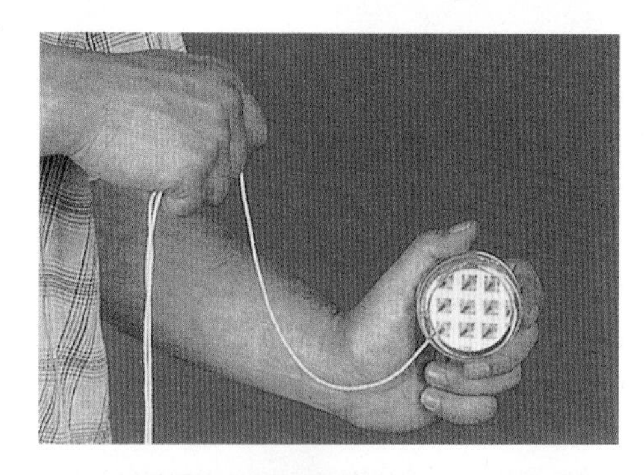

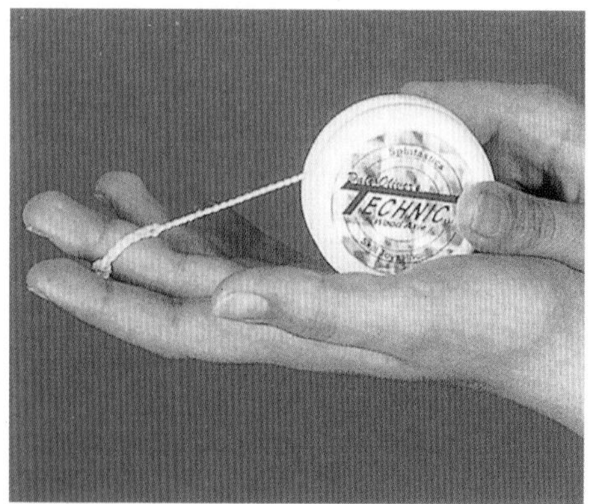

Yo-yo held the right way

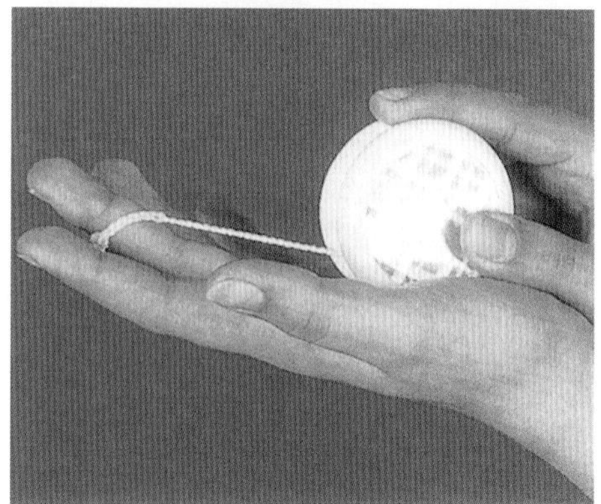

Yo-yo held the wrong way

Basic Throws

Gravity Pull

This is probably the first trick most beginning yo-yoers attempt.

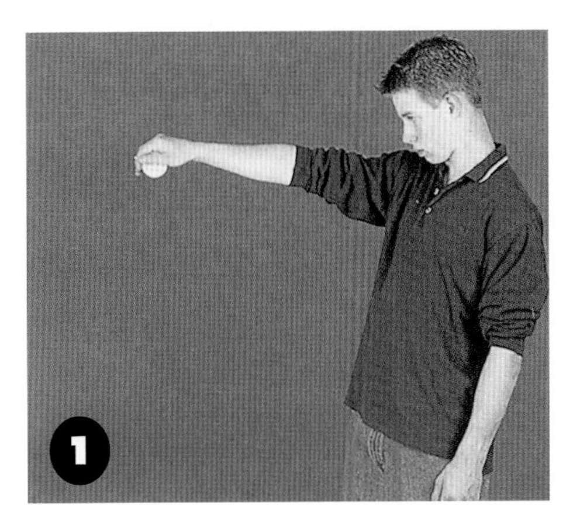

1. Hold the yo-yo in your hand with the palm facing down. Release the yo-yo and let it fall toward the floor.

2. As it travels on its downward journey, follow it down with your hand.

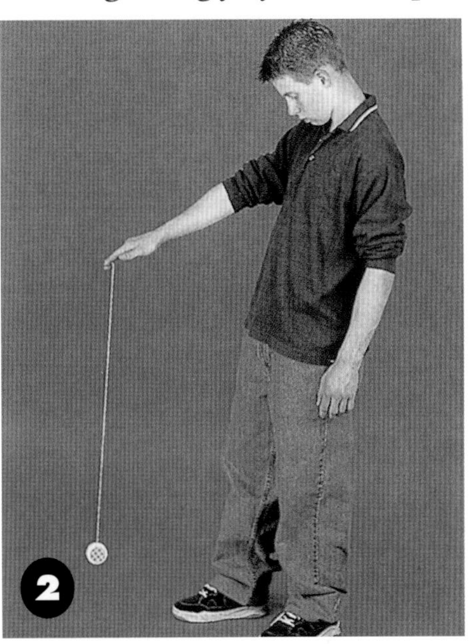

3. Just before the yo-yo gets to the bottom of the string, raise your hand. This will make the yo-yo climb back up the string. When it gets to the top, catch it.

Alternatively, instead of catching it, see how many times you can make it go up and down. This trick is called the Dribble.

Basic Power Throw

1. Cup the yo-yo in your palm and lift your elbow high enough that it is even with your eyes.

2. Throw your arm forward and let the yo-yo roll off the end of your fingers. Do not turn your hand over until the yo-yo is completely out of your hand.

3. Turn your palm downward, and lift your string finger. The yo-yo will return to your hand.

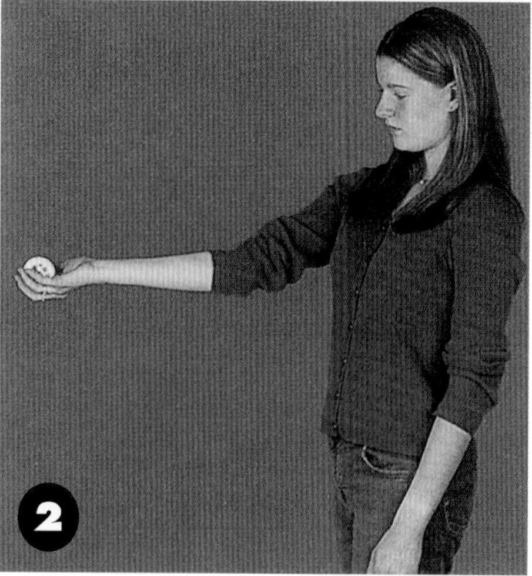

Remember: In all throws, use only one hand to catch the yo-yo. Try not to have any more than 3 inches (7.5 cm) of string left over between your yo-yo and your finger.

Sleeper or Spinner

Shakespeare once wrote "to sleep, perchance to dream," but not about playing with a yo-yo. This is one of the fundamental yo-yo throws.

Note: You can vary the length of time a yo-yo will sleep by the manner in which you throw it. The more powerful a throw, the longer it will sleep and the more it will spin at the bottom of the string. A gentle throw will result in a slower spin at the bottom of the string.

1. First check the tension of your string. If you think your yo-yo is too tight, hang it and give it several spins to the left (remember right-tight, left-loose). This trick works best with a loose string and a looser loop on the axle.

2. Cup the yo-yo in your palm and lift your elbow high enough that it is even with your eyes.

3. Throw your arm forward and drop the yo-yo. Your yo-yo should be spinning at the bottom of the string.

4. When you want your yo-yo to return, turn your palm down, lift your string finger, and the yo-yo will return to your hand.

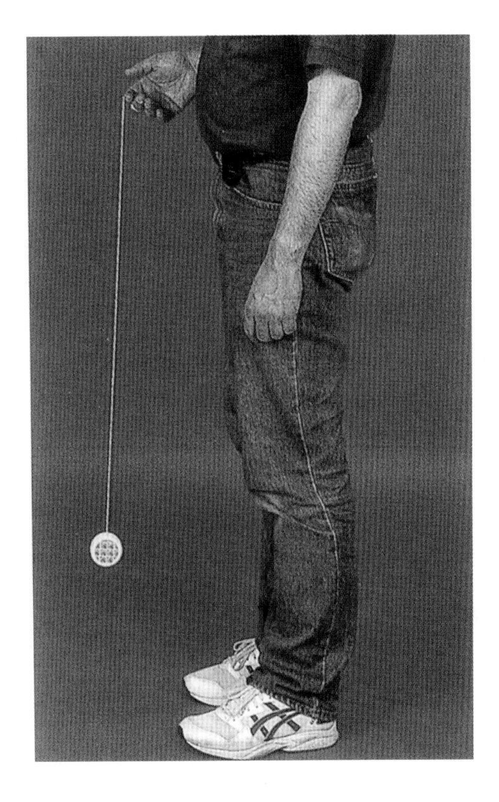

Forward Pass

Unlike a football quarterback, you won't have to worry about anyone catching this pass.

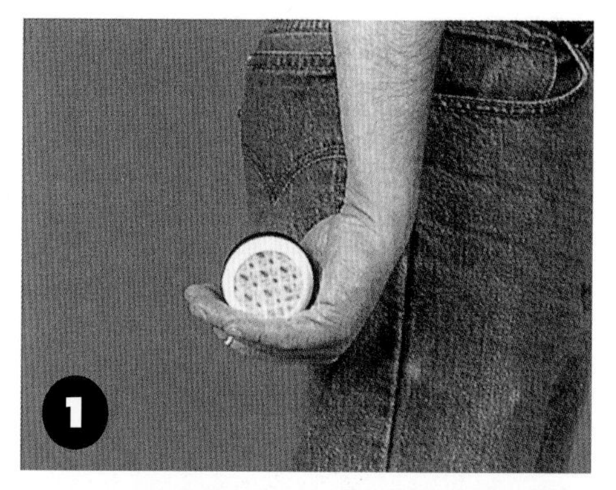

1. Cup the yo-yo in your palm loosely. Do not hold on to it. Make sure you keep your palm facing backward and your knuckles forward as you move your arm behind you. This is the same motion you use when you go on a brisk walk.

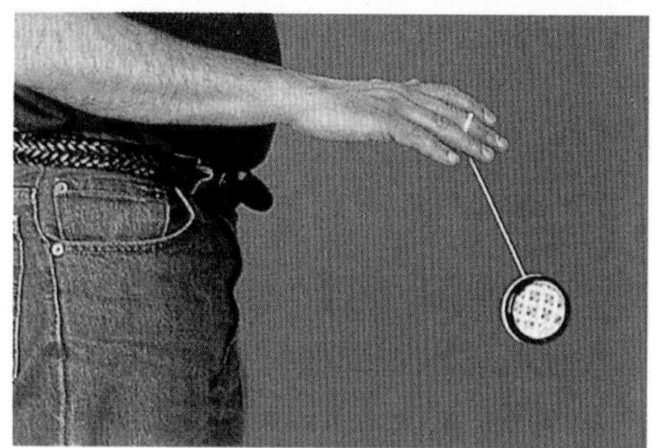

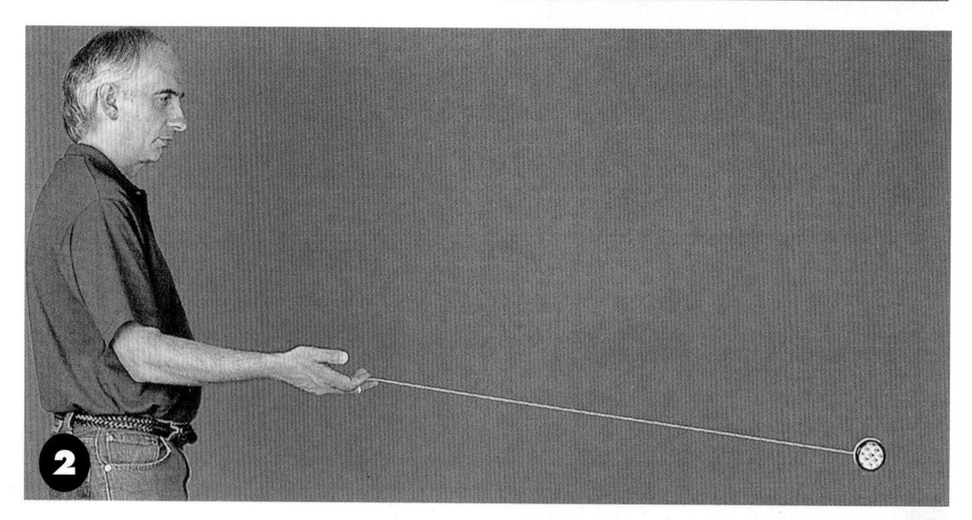

2. Release the yo-yo as you swing your arm forward. Bend your elbow slightly at the same time, so your elbow ends up about waist level. Turn your palm upward.

3. The yo-yo will shoot out in front of you and return to your hand.

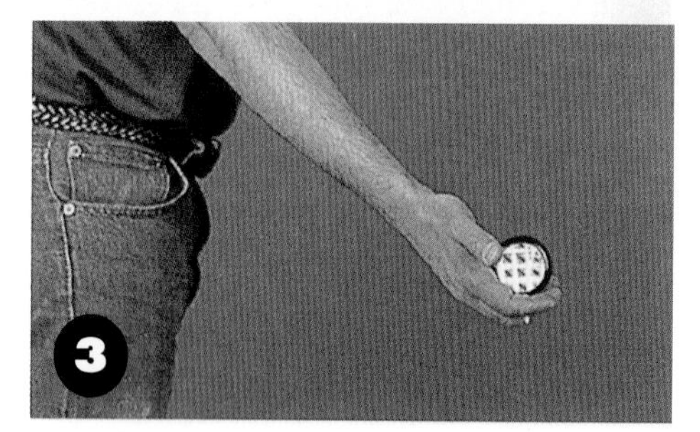

Loop the Loop

Not to get too loopy, but this is really fun to do.

1. Throw a forward pass.

2. Just before the yo-yo returns to your hand (where you would normally catch it), twist or rotate your wrist to send the yo-yo forward again. It is the same wrist motion as when you wave at someone to come closer.

3. The yo-yo should pass on the inside of your body. Try to get one good loop. When you can do one, try doing two, then try for five. Keep doing this until you can do 20 in a row. Remember to practice only good loops. If you lose control of your loops, stop and start again.

4. As you get better, practice alternating the loops. Do one repetition with the yo-yo on the inside of your body, with the next on the outside of your body.

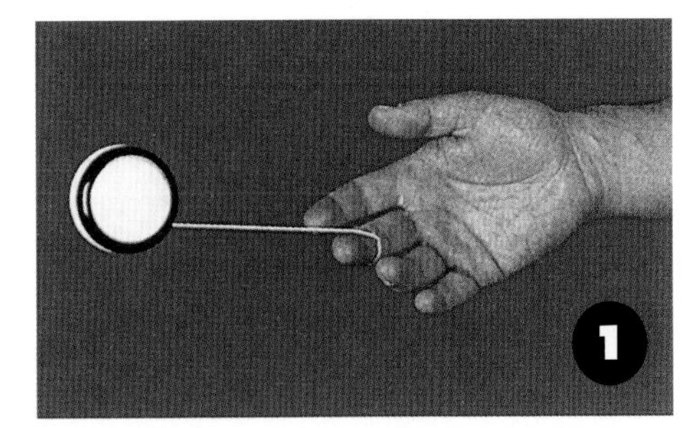

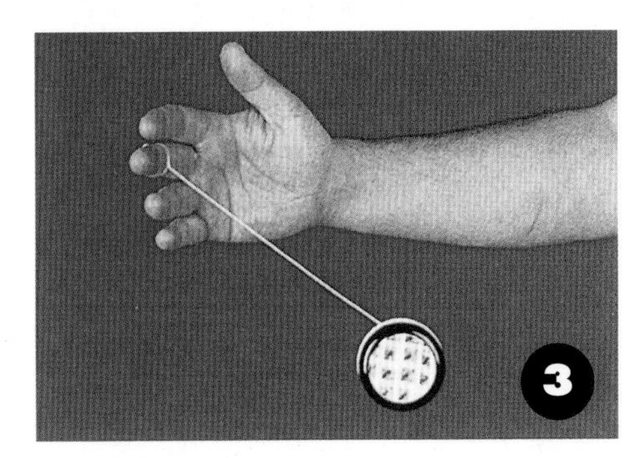

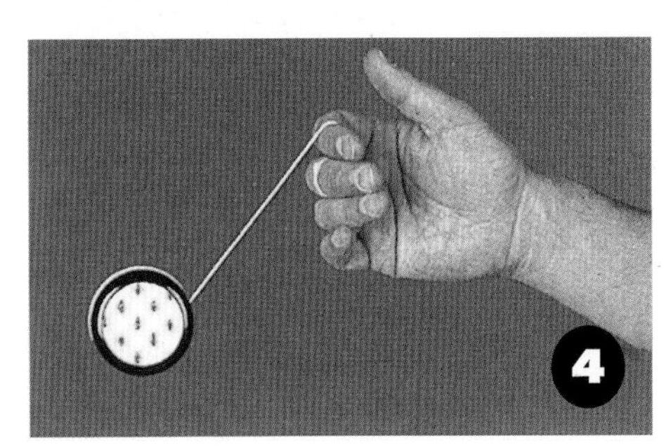

Note: In competitions, Loop the Loop is frequently used to break ties. Competitors can do 200 or more in a row.

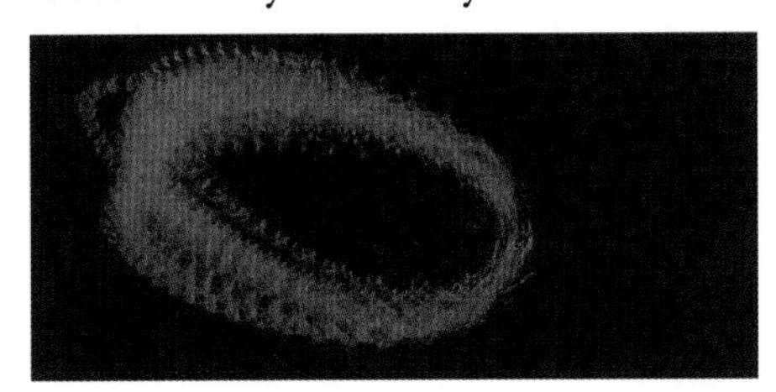

Loop the Loop with a strobe yo-yo

Beginner Tricks

Rock the Baby

There are a number of versions of this trick. This one is the simplest way of doing this classic. Some people mistakenly call this "Rock the Cradle." We'll show you that version, too.

1. Throw a fast Sleeper. You need to keep it sleeping long enough to do this trick.

2. Hold your yo-yo hand out as if you were asking someone to "stop." You should have a flat palm facing forward with the yo-yo string against your palm.

3. Take your free hand and pull the string between your first finger and thumb of your yo-yo hand, toward your body.

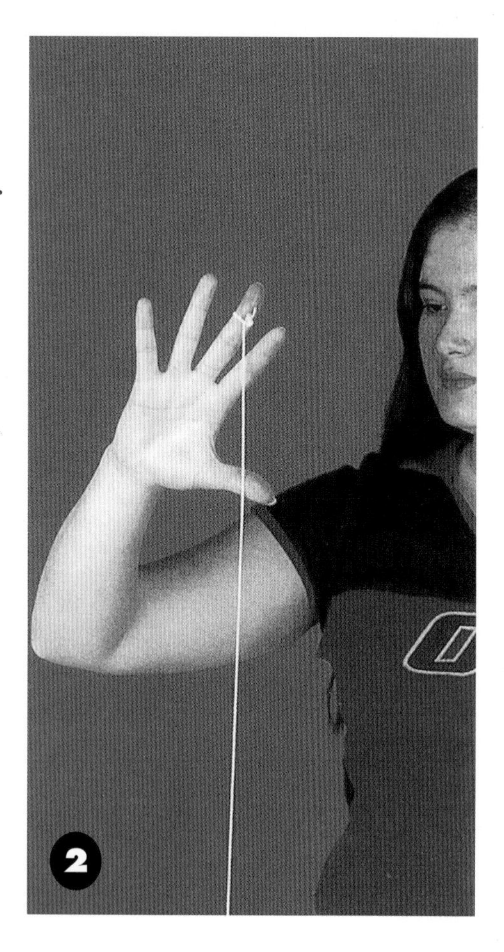

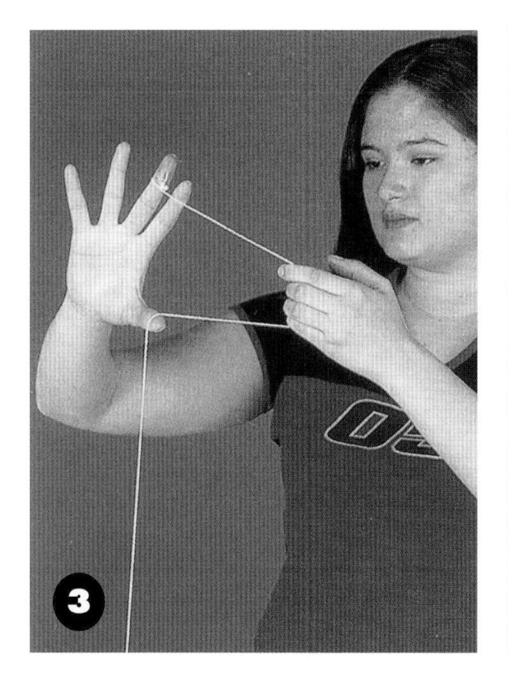

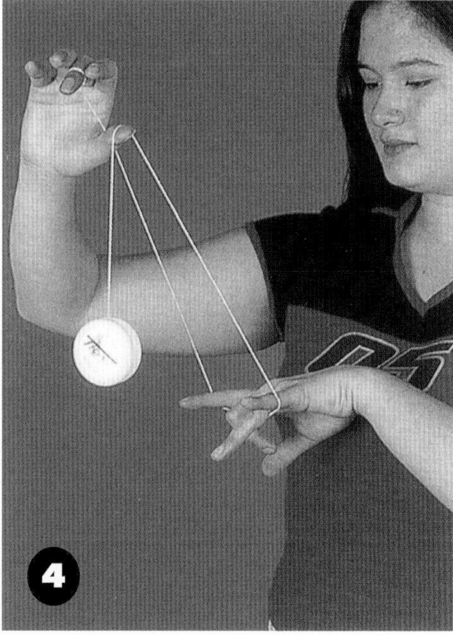

4. Use your fingers on your free hand to split open the string into a triangle shape. It should be wide enough for the yo-yo to be able to swing freely between the strings. You can size the cradle easily using this method, so you will always have sufficient space in which to swing. Move your top hand slightly to cause the yo-yo to move in and out of the triangle shape. This is the "rock."

5. After several passes through the archway release the string, and the yo-yo will wind up into your hand.

The Famous "Rock the Cradle"

Perhaps it's because the English language is such a precise tool that this trick was created.

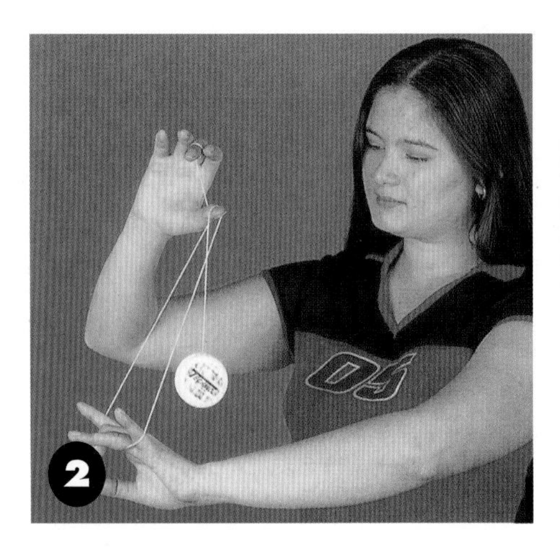

1. Complete all the steps in "Rock the Baby," but do not move the yo-yo in and out of the archway.

2. Instead, use your bottom or free yo-yo hand to move the triangle back and forth.

Hop the Fence

You won't have any major physical exertion with this next trick. Your wrist will substitute for a picket fence.

1. Do a basic power throw.

2. Instead of catching the yo-yo as it returns to your hand, slightly flick your wrist forward, as if you were pushing on a joystick, so the yo-yo does a flip and is propelled back down the string.

3. Practice till you can do this 10 times in a row. Catch the yo-yo on the last flip.

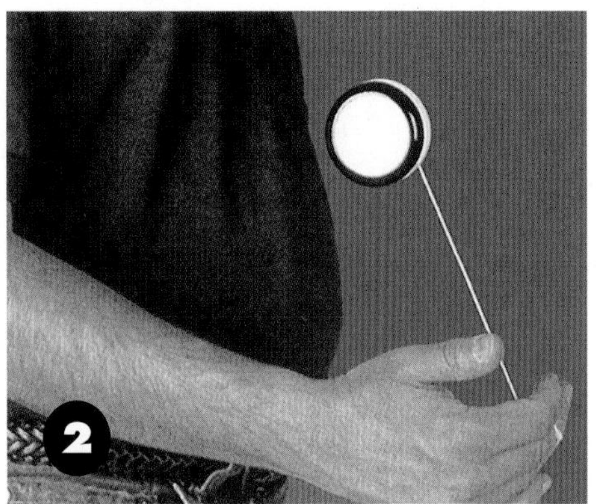

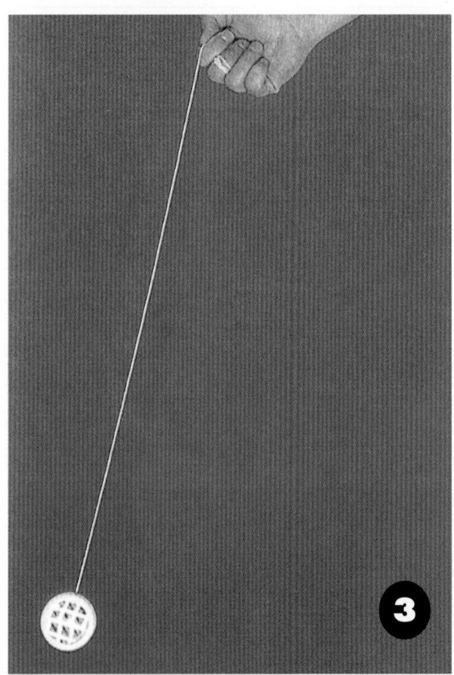

Walk the Dog

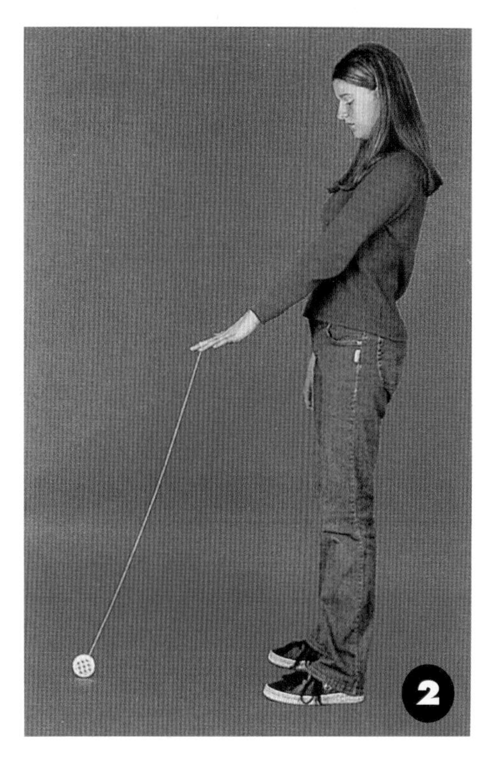

Here's one pet you won't mind taking out.

1. Throw a basic Sleeper. You might want to throw a fast one as it will work better.

2. When the yo-yo begins to sleep, bend forward slightly and allow the yo-yo to just touch the ground.

3. Keeping the yo-yo string taut, move your hand slowly forward, allowing the yo-yo to spin along the ground.

4. When the yo-yo has traveled about a foot or so away from you, yank the string and catch the yo-yo in your hand.

Breakaway

Your yo-yo may look as if it were trying to make a run for it, but unless your string breaks, this one will come back!

1. Make a muscle (like a weight lifter) by lifting your arm sideways. Your elbow should be even with your shoulder and the yo-yo should rest on your shoulder. Curve your wrist downward away from you.

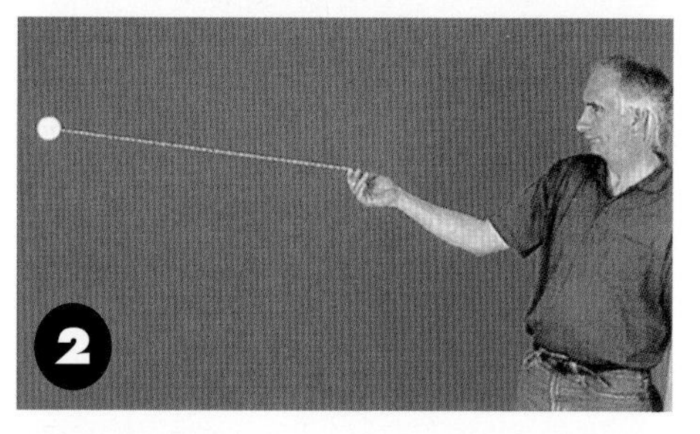

2. Flip your arm straight, releasing the yo-yo as you do this. The yo-yo will swing out and should now be soundly sleeping.

3. In one smooth motion, your hand will naturally move downward, then across your body. The weight of the yo-yo will cause it to swing across in front of your body.

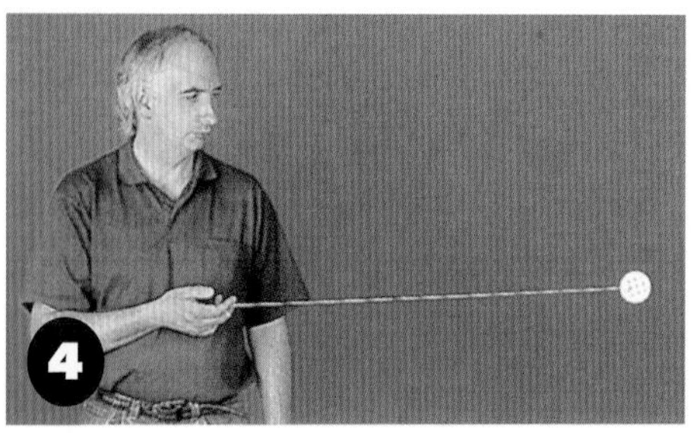

4. As the yo-yo completes its arc, give the string a tug with your yo-hand and it will snap back into your hand.

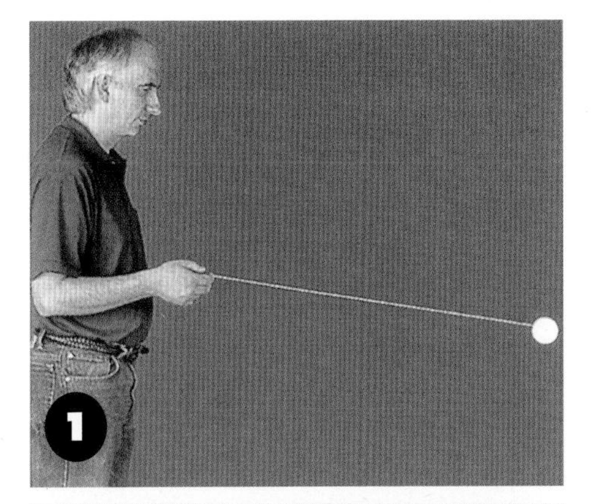

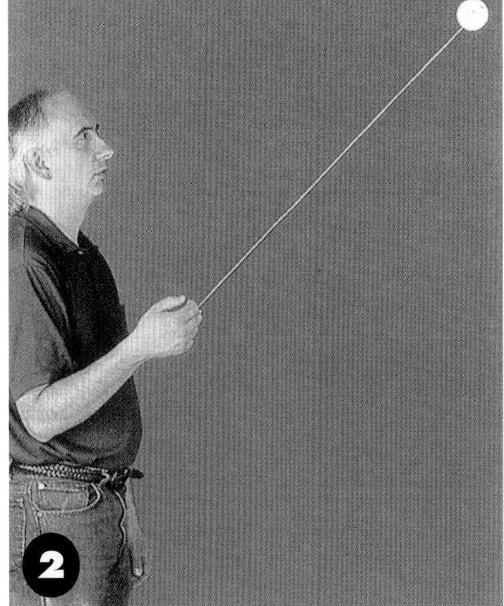

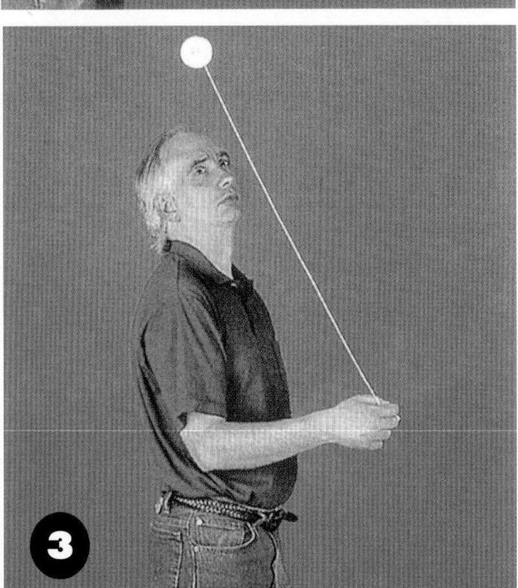

Around the World

In his classic book, Around the World in Eighty Days, *Jules Verne described the difficulties of making a journey such as this. You won't have half the problems his characters did, as you attempt to do such a feat with a yo-yo.*

REMEMBER: Look up and check for low-lying light fixtures before doing this trick.

1. This first step may seem counter-intuitive—that is to say, it may seem to make no sense and may go against what you'd normally think of doing. Throw a hard Forward Pass aiming slightly downward. Your yo-yo should be sleeping.

2. Pretend you're walking. Swing your arms in a natural motion, with the palm of your hand facing behind you. Just as you are moving your arm from back to front, let go of the yo-yo.

3. When your arm has reached the front of your body, stop your swing and allow the yo-yo to continue its journey around the world. You don't need to move your arm in a circular motion as if you were doing a "back stroke" in swimming.

4. When the yo-yo has completed its loop, give it a small yank to return it to your hand.

Advanced

By now you've impressed your friends and family with your new-found talent. You're ready for some more challenging tricks.

Creeper

This is not a trick involving climbing ivy, nor is it a scary movie. It's a variation of Walk the Dog, but your string will be parallel to the ground. Here are two of the several versions of this trick:

1. Throw a basic fast Sleeper.

2.. When the yo-yo begins to sleep, swing the yo-yo out in front of you and let it land gently on the floor.

3. Give the string a tug, and the yo-yo will come back. Remember that the yo-yo must stay on the floor for its entire trip back to your hand.

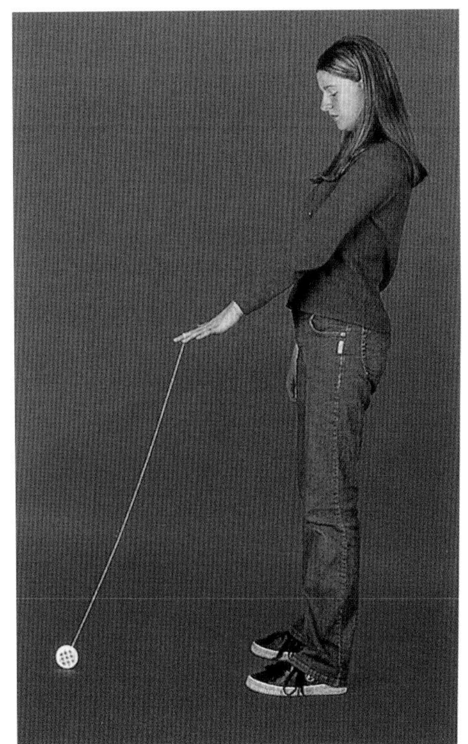

Creeper II

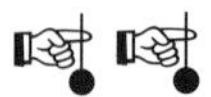

This second variation is commonly called Land Rover.

1. Throw a basic fast Sleeper.

2. This time when the yo-yo begins to sleep, bend forward at the waist and knees until your hand is just above the floor. The yo-yo should be scooting along the ground away from you.

3. As the yo-yo reaches the end of the string, give it a tug, and it will come shuffling back.

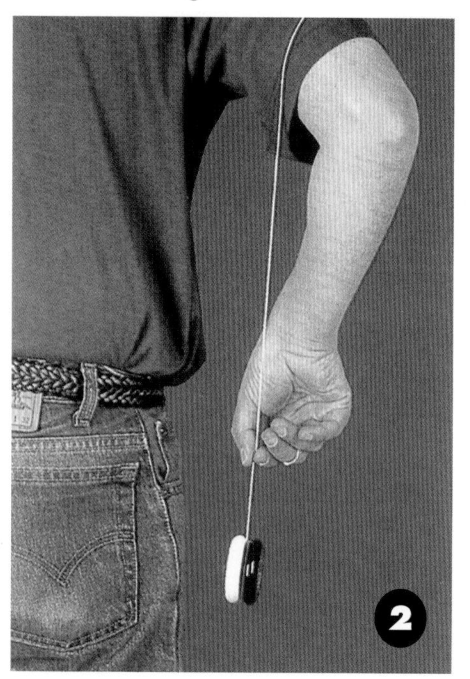

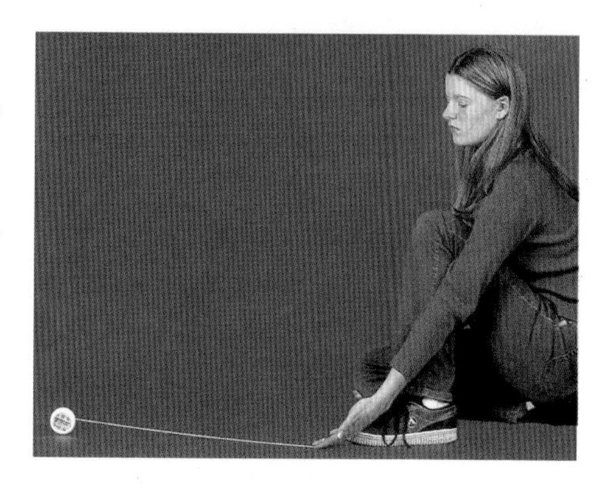

Around the Corner (also known as Over the Shoulder)

This one looks great. If you do this in a competition, make sure to roll your sleeve so the yo-yo doesn't get caught in the material.

1. Throw a basic fast Sleeper.

2. Lift your hand straight up and allow the yo-yo string to go behind you and rest on your shoulder.

3. Lean slightly forward so your fingers on your yo-yo hand can touch the string on your shoulder.

4. "Pluck" or tweak the string and the yo-yo will climb back up the string, flip over your shoulder, and land back in your hand.

Over the Falls

There's no water involved here.

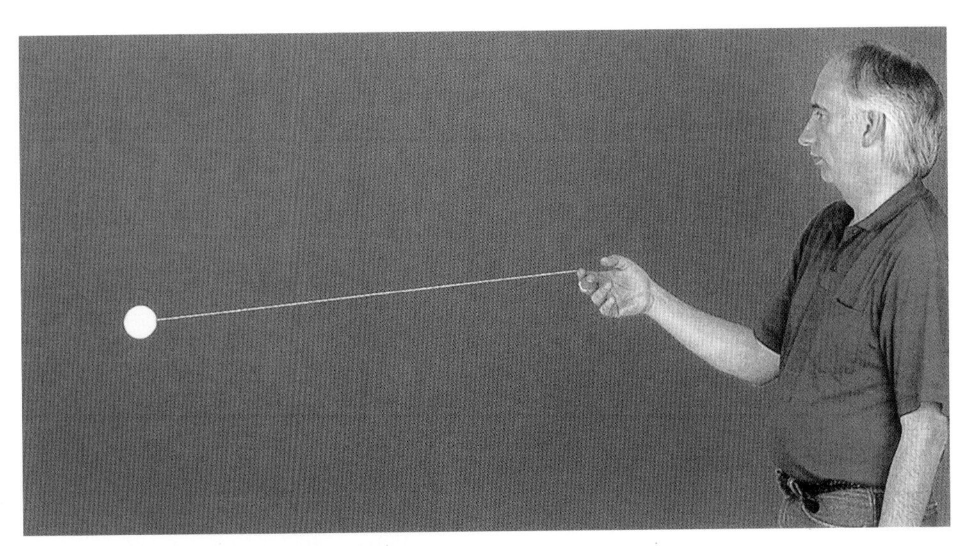

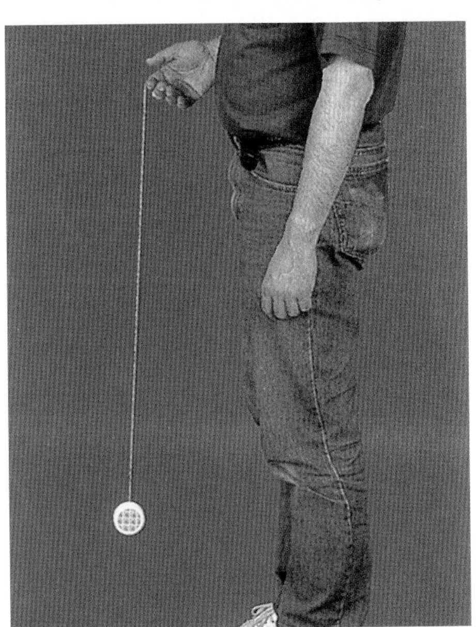

1. Throw a Forward Pass. Remember to use the same arm motion you would if you were swinging your arms while walking.

2. Before the yo-yo gets back to your hand, curve your wrist and allow the yo-yo to drop to the ground.

3. Catch the yo-yo as it returns to your hand.

Punching Bag

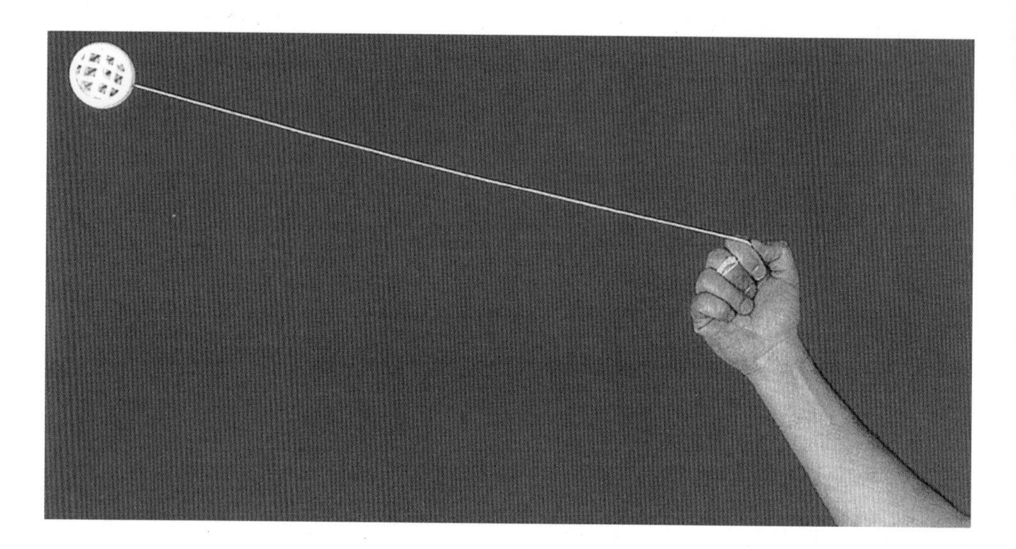

Boxers practice by hitting a punching bag. It looks like a puffy basketball hung on a string and suspended above the ground at head height. Here's the yo-yo equivalent. This trick is to make the yo-yo do something it doesn't want to. It has to do a reverse loop. The yo-yo has to go in a direction from the top of the yo-yo toward the bottom, as opposed to bottom or under the hand, as in Loop the Loop.

1. Check the tension on your string. You want it tight, so the yo-yo doesn't sleep in the middle of this trick. Begin by doing Hop the Fence. As the yo-yo hops over your hand, gradually raise your arm and force the hops to go in a horizontal direction in front of you. The secret is to already have good control when Hopping the Fence.

2. For a single trick, catch the yo-yo as it returns to you.

3. When you can perform this without any difficulty, try to keep the yo-yo punching the air repeatedly. Try doing two, then try for five. Keep doing this until you can do 20 in a row. Remember to practice only good loops. If you lose control of your loops, stop and start again. Keep in mind that this is one of the hardest looping tricks in existence, so don't feel bad if you can't get the hang of this right away.

Three-Leaf Clover

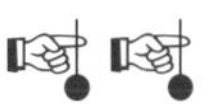

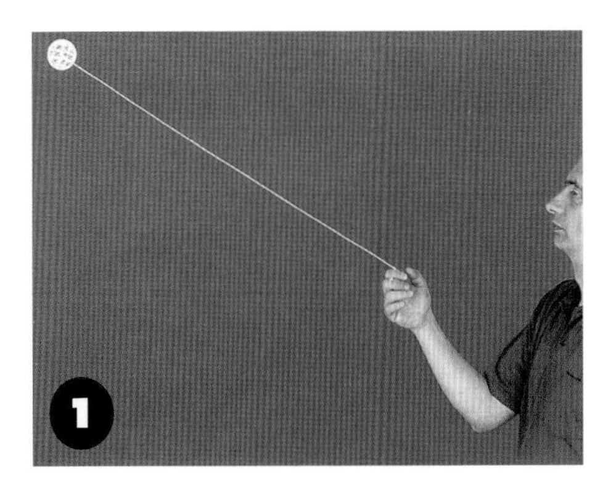

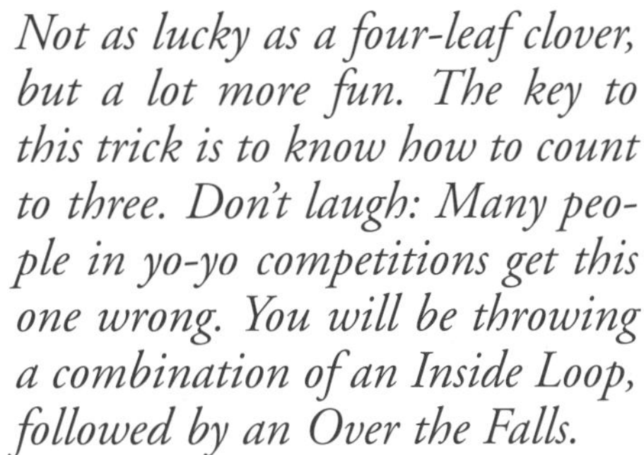

Not as lucky as a four-leaf clover, but a lot more fun. The key to this trick is to know how to count to three. Don't laugh: Many people in yo-yo competitions get this one wrong. You will be throwing a combination of an Inside Loop, followed by an Over the Falls.

1. Check the tension on your string. You want it tight, so the yo-yo doesn't sleep in the middle of this trick. Instead of throwing a Loop in front of you, aim upward at about a 45-degree angle, then throw your Loop. This is the first leaf.

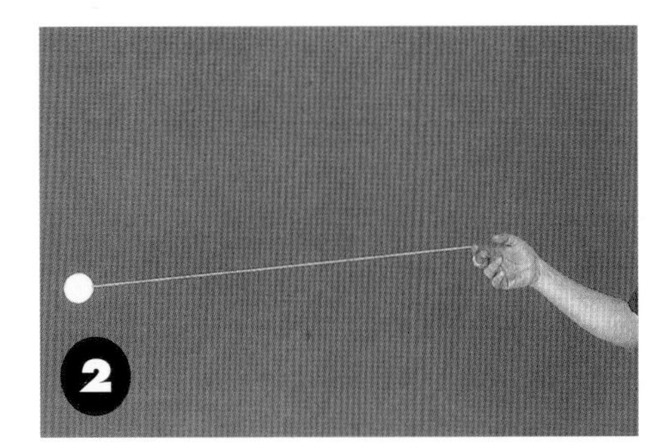

2. This next step is basically the same as Over the Falls. As the yo-yo returns, flip your wrist so the yo-yo does a turn and heads straight out from your body. This is the second leaf.

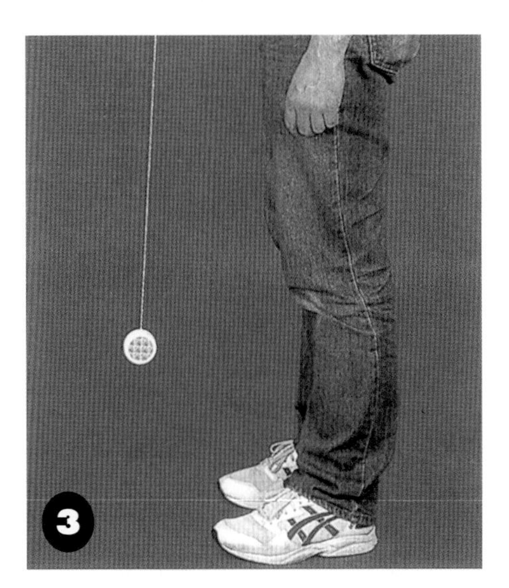

3. Just as the yo-yo returns, flip your wrist again and head the yo-yo toward the floor. This is the third leaf. Catch the yo-yo when it comes up. Try to make the yo-yo go straight down on this last leaf.

Flying Saucer
(Sleeping Beauty)

☞☞

As you use your yo-yo, the string gets tighter or looser. One way to adjust this tension is to perform this trick.

1. Place your arms at a 45-degree angle to the side of your body. Throw a Sleeper at this angle.

2. When the yo-yo is sleeping, use your finger to draw up the yo-yo string to a horizontal position in front of your body.

3. The yo-yo will begin to "vibrate" or spin sideways (horizontal to the ground). You will actually see the string spinning sideways around the yo-yo.

4. Give the string a slight tweak up with your free hand. As you do, the string will wind back up into the yo-yo.

Lariat

☞☞

You won't catch any horses with this variation on the Flying Saucer, but you should be able to rope in your yo-yo.

1. Throw a Sleeping Beauty, but do not use your free hand to lift the yo-yo by the string.

2. Instead of grasping the string with your free hand, move your yo-yo hand from the 45-degree angle to a position directly above the yo-yo.

3. Pull the yo-yo straight up and move your hand to the side as it rises. You should see the string rotating around the yo-yo as you do this.

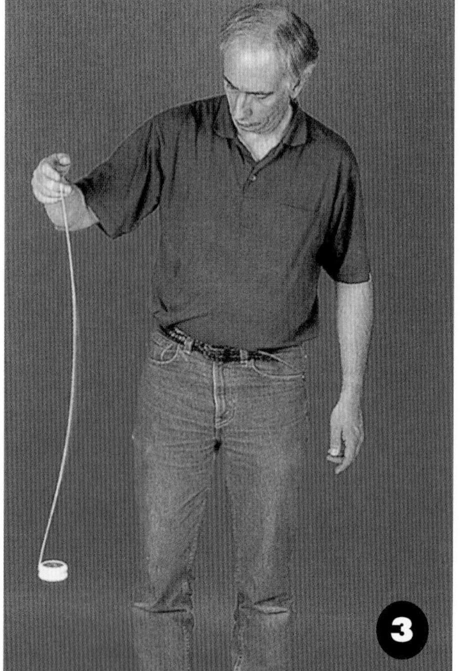

Man on the Flying Trapeze

This is a classic yo-yo trick—the quintessential string trick—and one that never fails to impress people. You may see yo-yo experts wearing one glove that looks eaten away by moths. The glove is used to cut down on rope burns from tricks such as this.

1. Throw a Breakaway.

2. With your free hand (the one without a yo-yo attached to it), put your pointer finger in a direct line with the arc of the yo-yo string. Make sure you put your finger about 2-3 inches (5-7.5 cm) away from the end of the yo-yo. If you do this too close, the yo-yo will bite your finger. If you are too far away, the yo-yo will probably miss the string and go around your finger.

3. The yo-yo will flip over your finger and land on the string.

4. Bring your hands slightly together, then pull them apart. As you do this, the yo-yo will "dismount" and wind back up into the toy. This is usually called the "flyaway dismount."

Rattlesnake

You won't get bitten by this snake, but you will really see why this trick is named after a reptile. It is recommended that you wear long pants while you perform this trick.

1. Throw a Lariat (see above).

2. As the string is oscillating above the yo-yo, bring the yo-yo back toward your leg.

3. Allow the string to barely touch your leg. This will give you the sound of a rattlesnake.

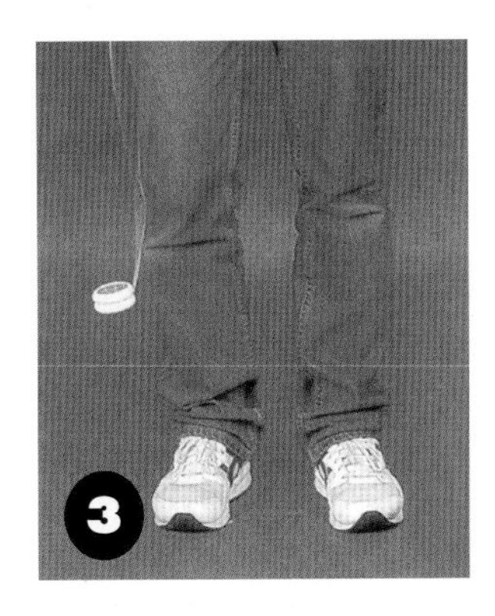

Double or Nothing

This trick gets its name because if you do the throw correctly it will loop twice, but if you miss, you end up with a dangling string—in other words—nothing.

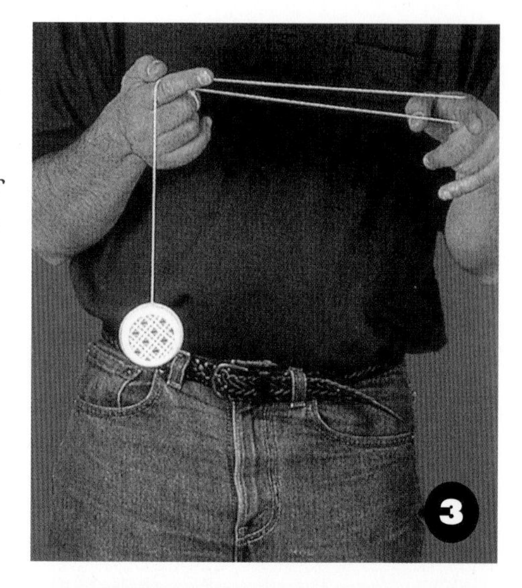

1. Throw a fast Breakaway.

2. As it completes its arc, place your finger out to the side (as you did in Man on the Flying Trapeze). Instead of catching the yo-yo on the string, allow the yo-yo to continue traveling until it reaches your yo-yo hand.

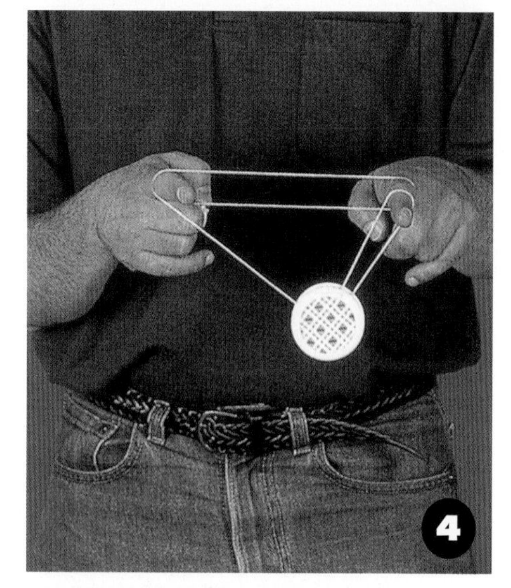

3. Point the index finger of your yo-yo hand outward and allow the yo-yo to swing over that finger.

4. As the yo-yo passes the yo-yo index finger allow it to catch onto the string and flip over. The forward momentum of the yo-yo should land on the string.

5. Release the yo-yo using a "Fly Away" dismount and catch it as it returns.

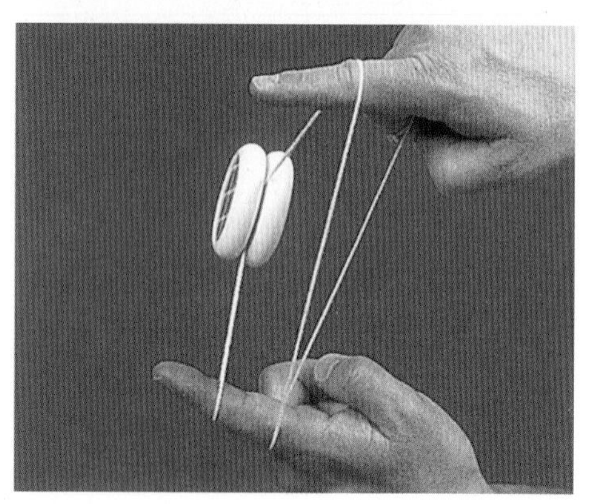

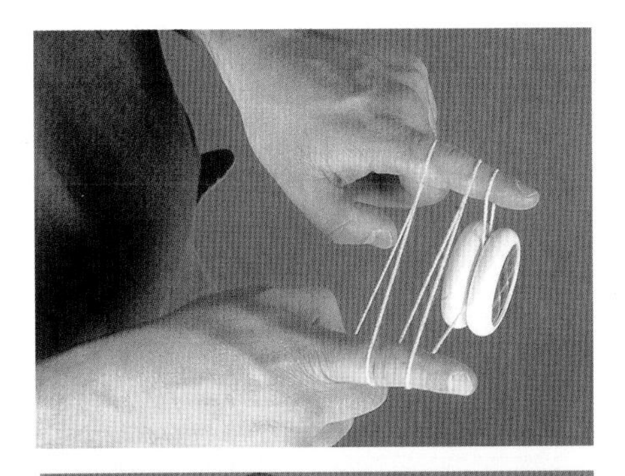

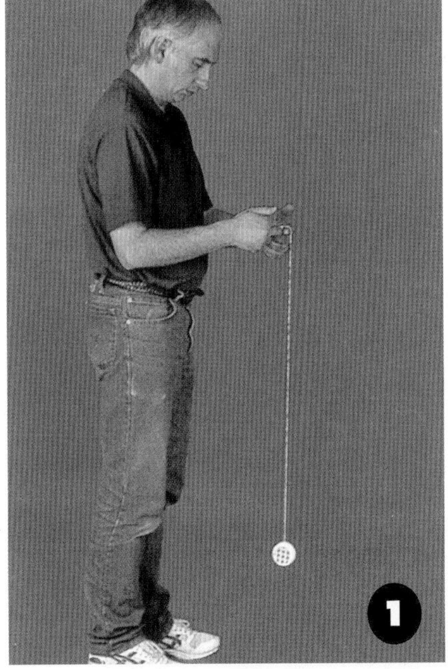

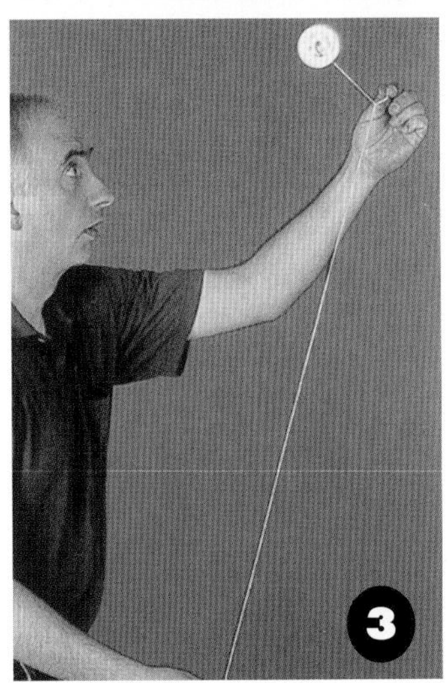

Triple or Nothing

Allow the yo-yo to continue one more rotation around your hand before catching it on the string. As in Double or Nothing, if you miss, you'll end up with a mass of string and a yo-yo going nowhere.

Hint: Each time the yo-yo wraps around your finger, the string should angle off the other end. The string should not be parallel when viewed from above. Remember that the yo-yo's final landing will be on the outside string.

Pinwheel

Pinwheels are something you normally use to catch the wind. This pinwheel won't do that, but you'll see why it is so named. There are a number of variations on this trick. This is the one asked for in competitions.

1. Throw a fast or strong Sleeper. This should be thrown directly in front of your body.

2. Using the thumbnail of your free hand, place the fingernail in front of the string. (Why the thumbnail, you may ask? To save you from string burn!)

3. Pull down with your yo-yo hand, and raise the yo-yo to about shoulder level.

4. Pinch the string with your thumb and index finger of your free hand.

5. This pinching, along with the spinning of the yo-yo, will allow the yo-yo to rotate several times around your hand.

6. Drop the yo-yo and it will return.

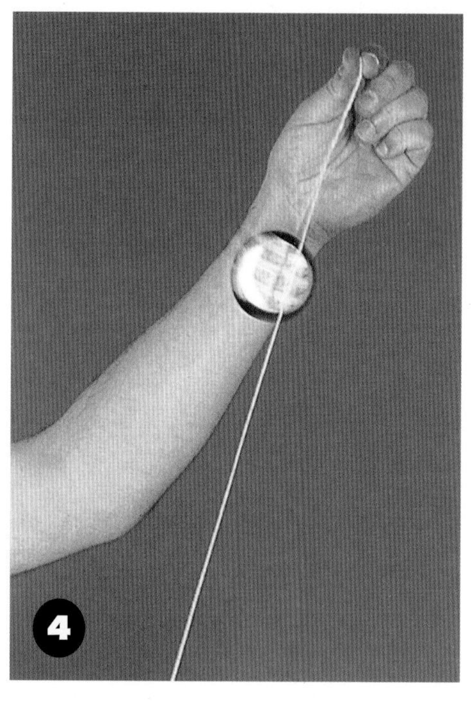

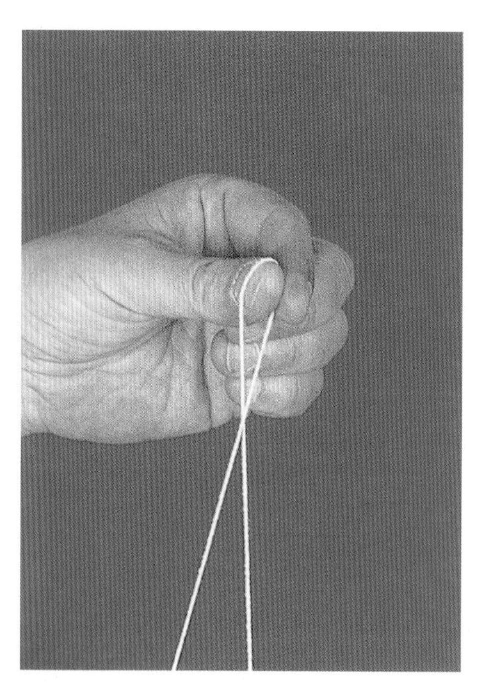

Variation:

If you don't pinch the yo-yo, but just allow it to rotate around your index finger, it will come off your thumb and onto the finger, then drop. This is called a "Pull Over."

Tidal Wave

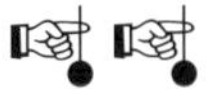

This is the new name for what has traditionally been known as "skin the cat," which, of course, no one should ever do. While tsunamis (large tidal waves) aren't much fun, Tidal Wave is a better name for the trick.

1. Throw a fast or hard Sleeper.

2. Place the pointer finger of your free hand behind the string. Pull the yo-yo hand back toward your side in a downward motion.

3. When your yo-yo gets to about chest level, give the string a light flip with your pointer finger. The yo-yo will pop up and return to your hand.

4. Instead of catching the yo-yo, give your wrist a twist and send the yo-yo outward. It will resemble a loop and will be at waist level, not ground level.

5. As it returns this time, catch the yo-yo in your hand.

Expert

Reach for the Moon

This tough trick gets its name because it is as ambitious as reaching for the moon.

1. Start with a Forward Pass, but aim this one about 45 degrees up, so your throwing hand is about as high as your nose.

2. As the yo-yo returns to your hand, give your wrist a slight flick, so the yo-yo passes under your hand and continues up and behind you.

3. When the yo-yo comes back down and is about the same level as your hand, give your hand a forward wrist flick and send the yo-yo back up into the air in front of you.

4. If you are just doing one repetition, catch the yo-yo on its return. Remember one repetition is "front, back, front, catch."

5. If you are doing several repetitions, keep flicking your wrist as you did in steps 2 and 3. Expert yo-yoers can do at least 10 of these in a row.

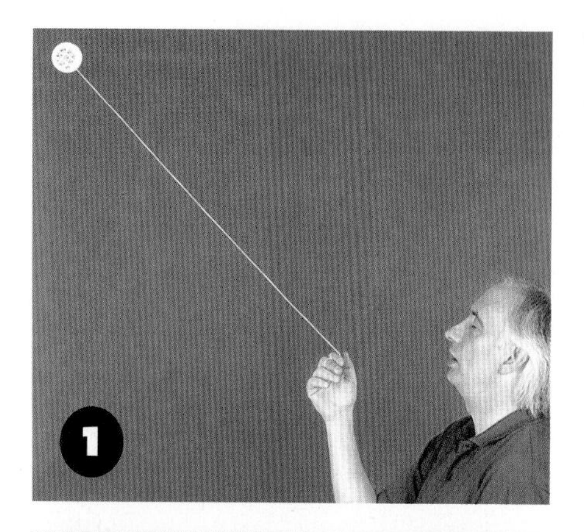

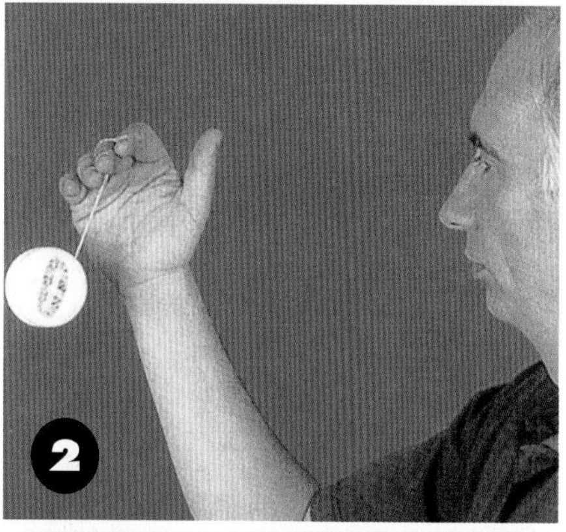

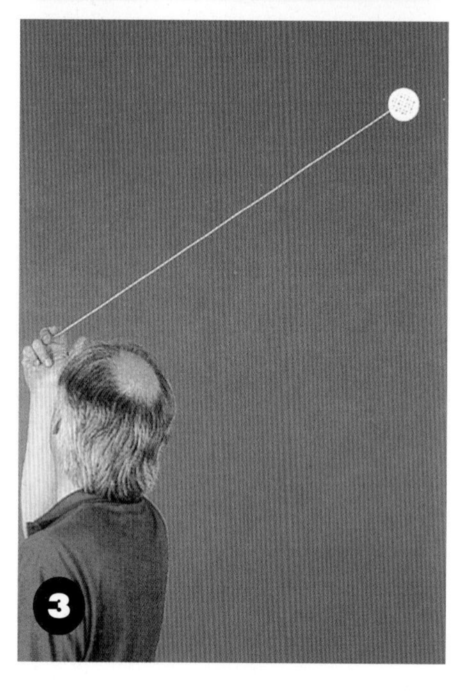

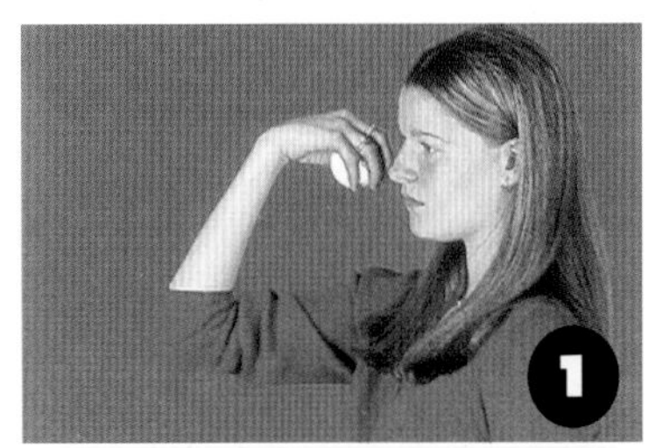

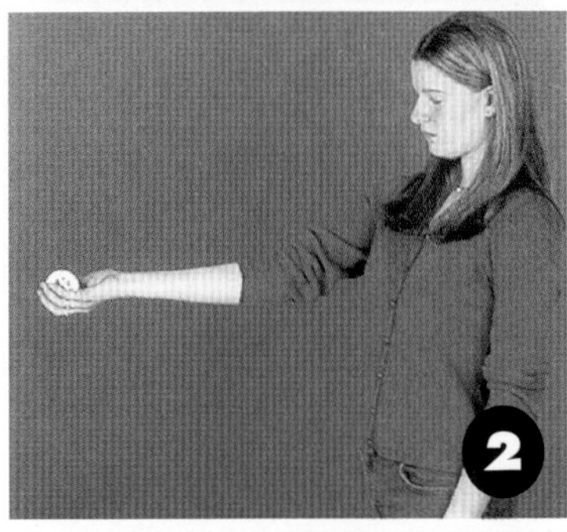

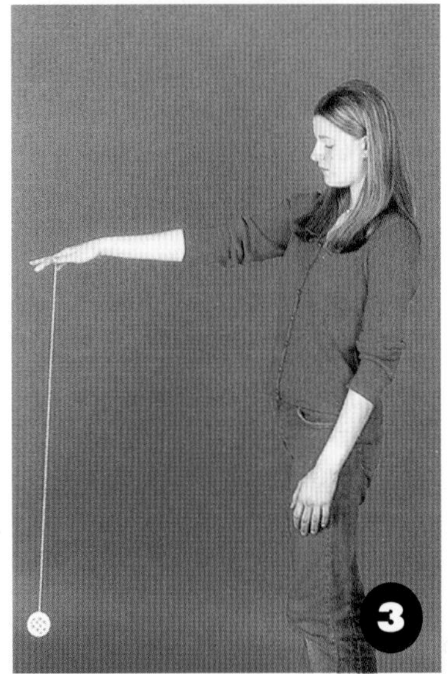

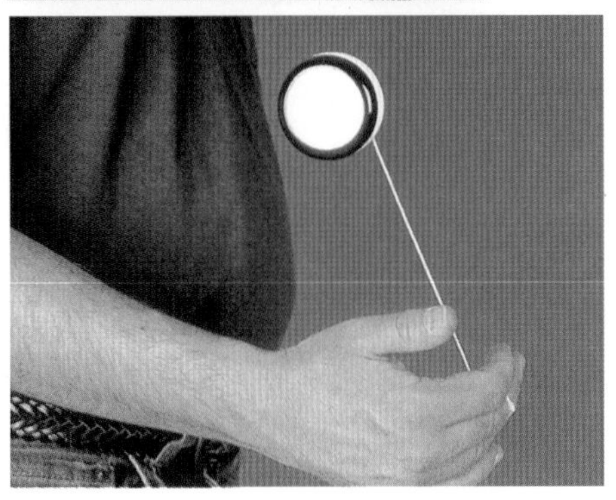

Planet Hop

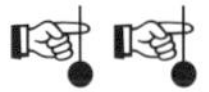

On the subject of objects in space, here's another one that's out of this world. Don't confuse this with Hop the Fence.

1. Start with your Basic Power Throw.

2. As the yo-yo returns to your hand, allow the yo-yo to hop over the top of your hand.

3. When the yo-yo comes back up again, give it a slight flick (as in Hop the Fence) and it will jump back over your hand. One repetition is "front, back, front, catch." Hop the Fence is a loop going in only one direction. Planet Hop alternates between front and back.

4. Try to see how many good reps you can do in a row. Remember to start over when you lose control.

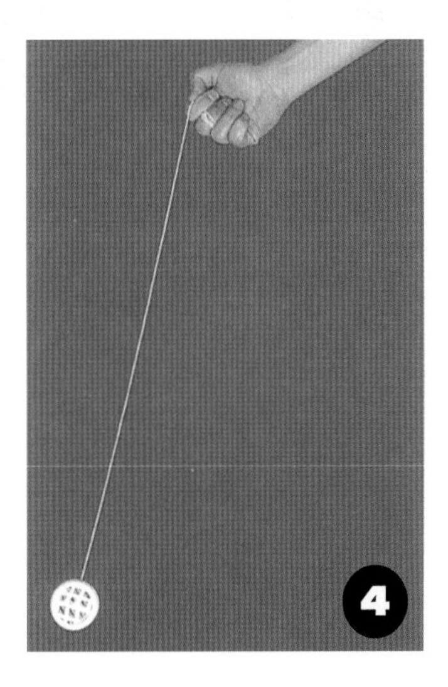

Brain Twister

Wrap you mind around the next trick. A word of advice: Wear a glove and keep your free hand as steady as possible.

1. Throw a fast or hard Sleeper.

2. Place the index finger of your free hand about halfway down the yo-yo string.

3. Pull back to lift the yo-yo with your finger so it is about even with your chest.

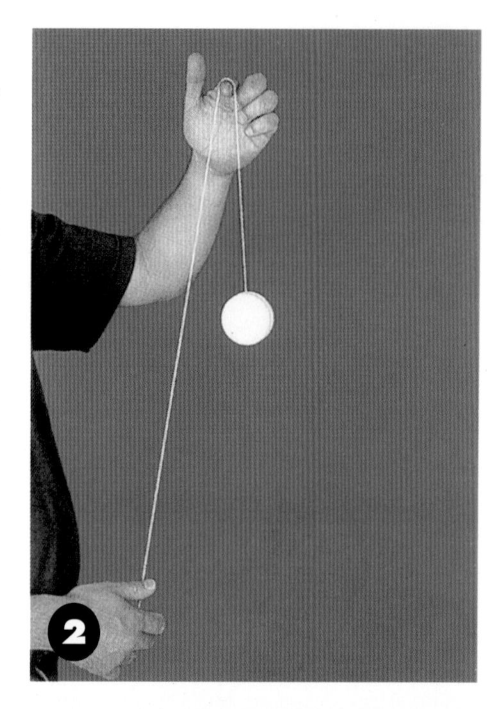

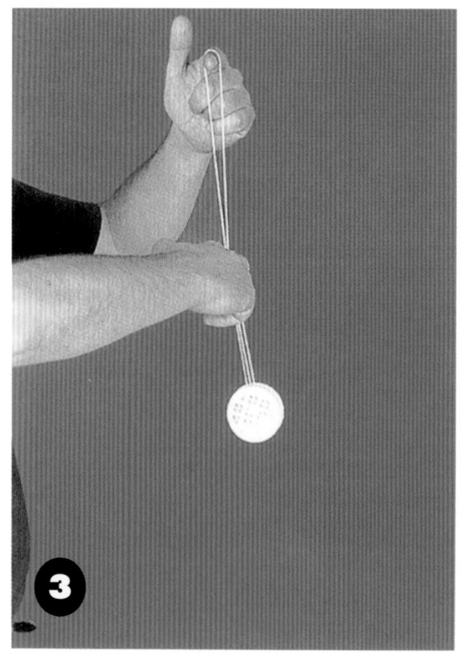

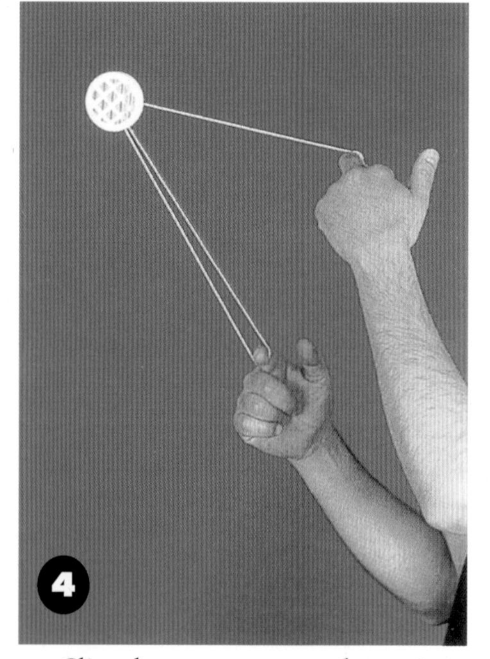

4. Slip the yo-yo onto the string, about halfway between this finger and the finger to which the yo-yo is attached.

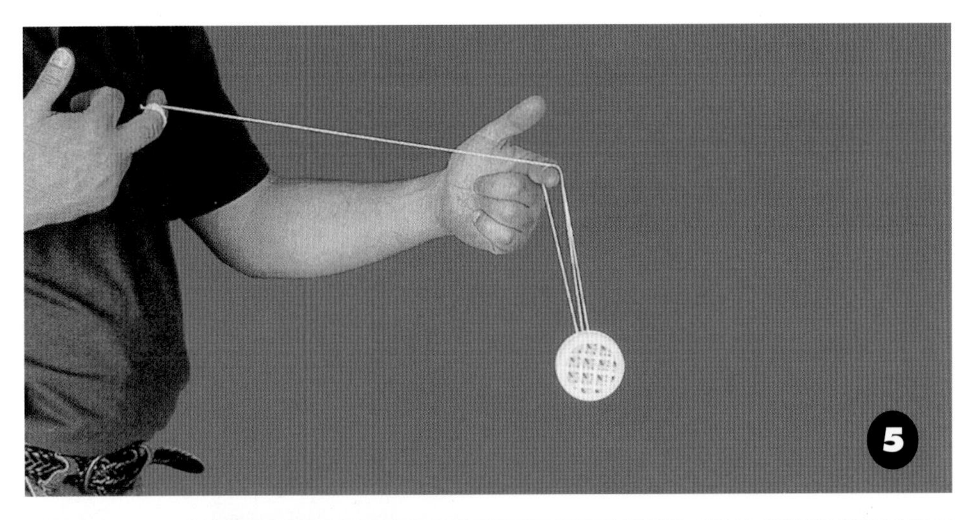

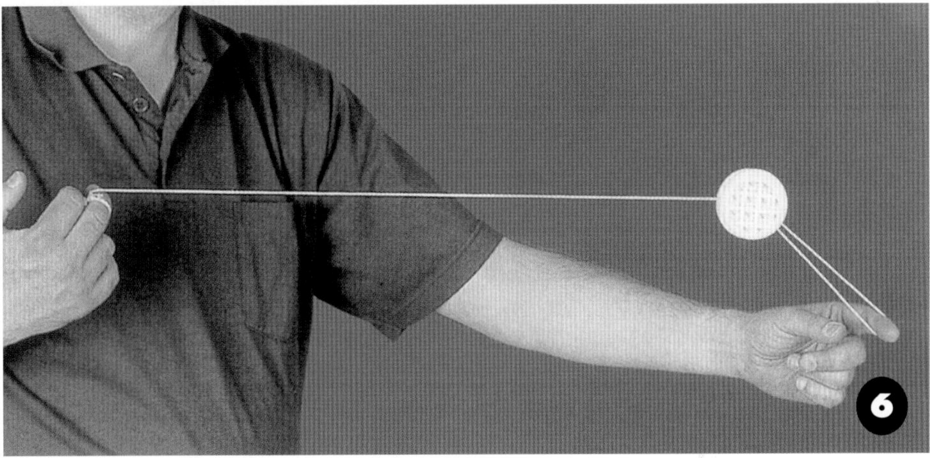

5. Adjust the length of string by bringing your yo-yo hand about halfway between the yo-yo and your non-yo-yo finger.

6. Use your yo-yo finger to push back into the double string and guide the yo-yo, so that it somersaults over your non-yo-yo finger.

7. Pull back with your yo-yo hand and release the yo-yo, so that it rolls off and returns to your hand.

Atom Smasher

If you had a particle accelerator handy you could use it, but a yo-yo will work just fine. This is the toughest one-handed string trick you will have to do in most competitions. Good luck! By the way: this is the basic version—there are harder ones.

1. Throw a fast or hard Sleeper.

2. Place the index finger of your free hand about halfway down the yo-yo string. Pull back to lift the yo-yo with your finger until it is about waist level.

3. Tuck your yo-yo finger into the palm of your hand, then use your index finger to flip the yo-yo string onto the finger. The yo-yo will hop over your finger and onto the string. This is called a "split bottom entry." Do not punch the string as you will probably miss the hop. The weight of the yo-yo will be enough to carry it forward.

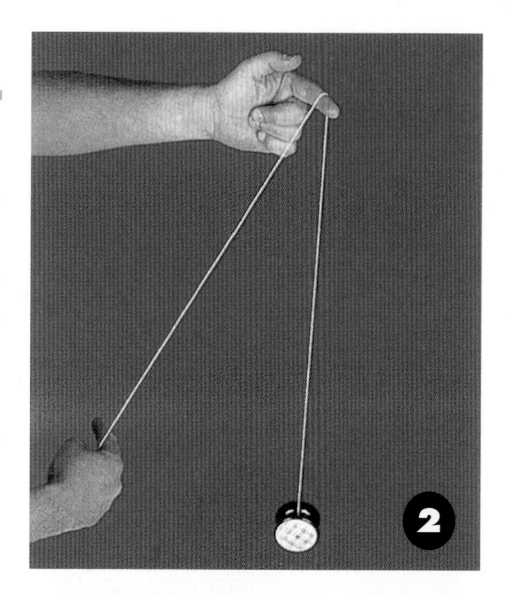

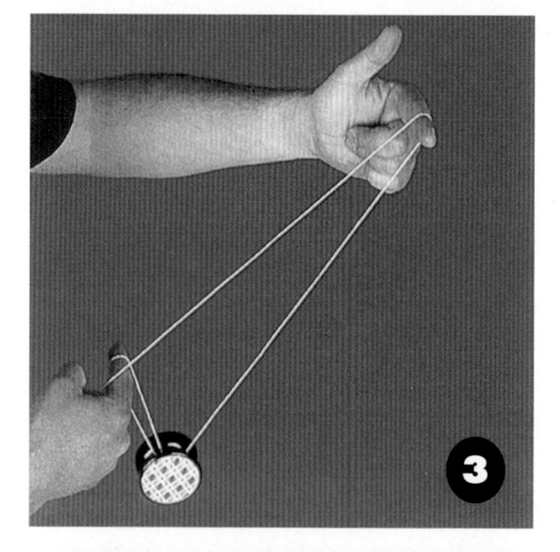

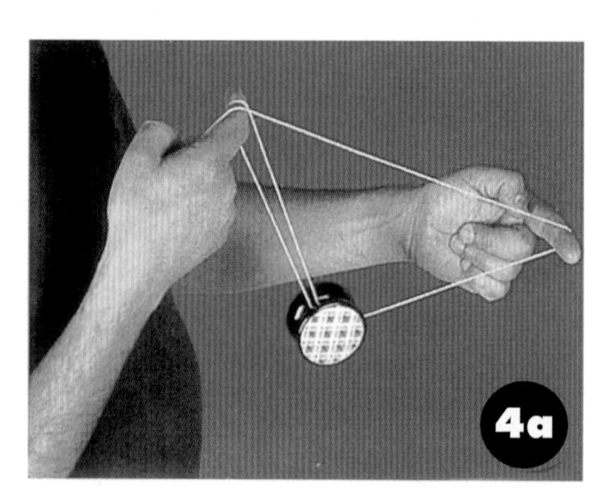

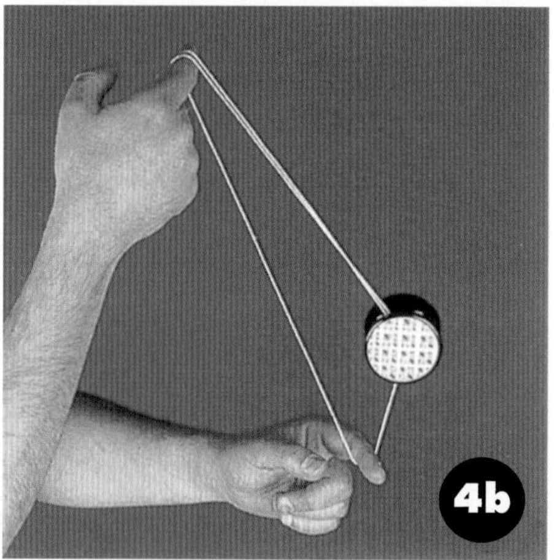

4. With the index finger of your free hand on the inside loop of the yo-yo, follow the string around under the yo-yo, going front to back. This is called a "pass under."

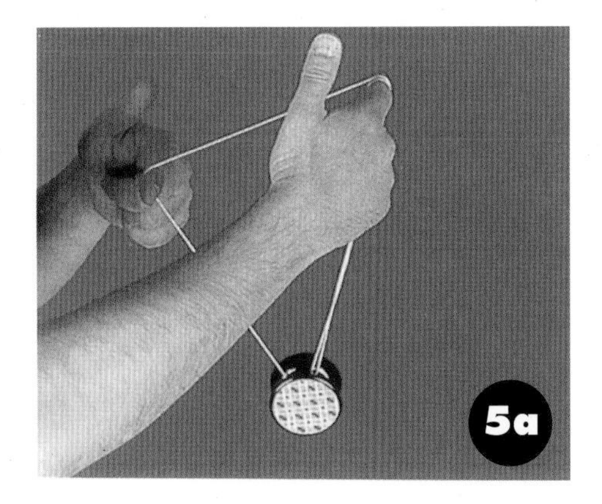

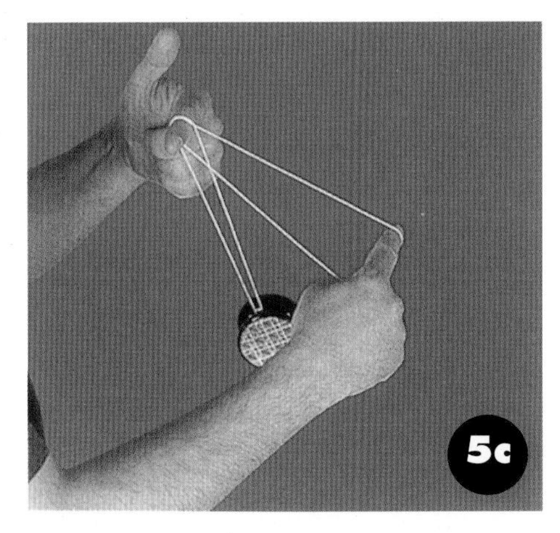

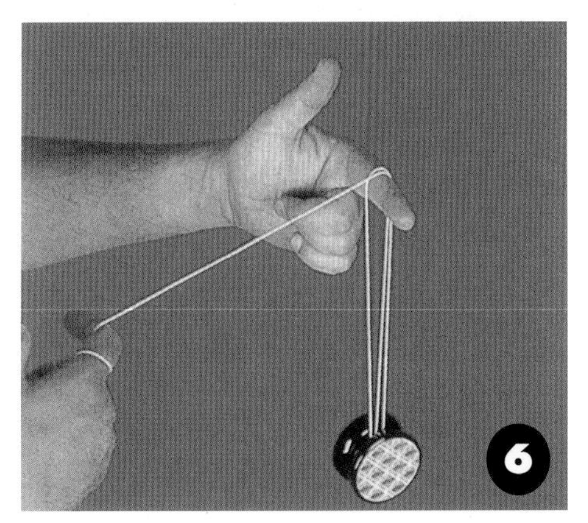

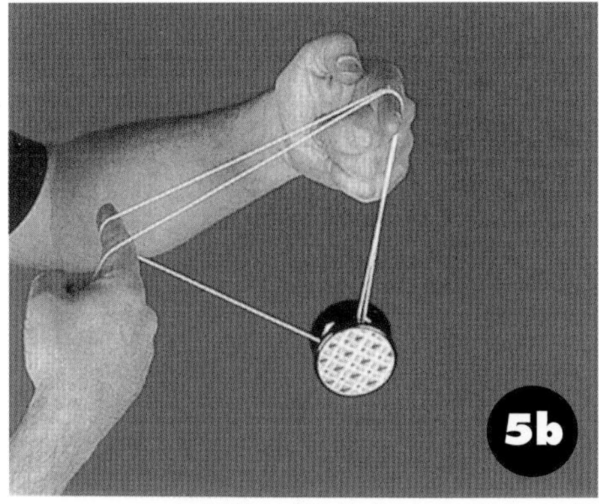

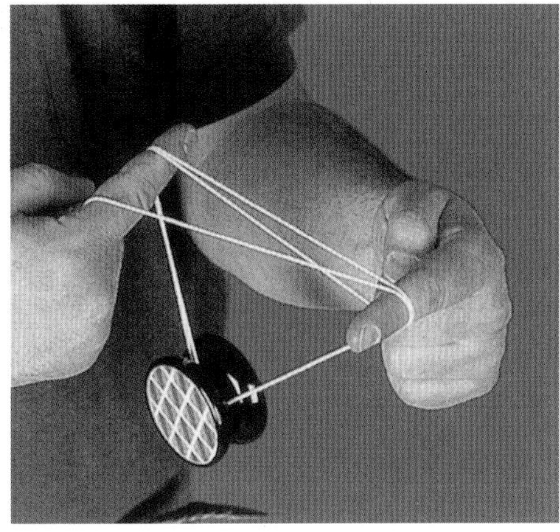

5. When your finger is at about the halfway point on the string closest to you, move it straight across or forward, into the double string. Take the single string, which your yo-yo hand is holding, and pass it under the yo-yo in a back-to-front direction.

6. Punch your finger back into the double string, which will give you another somersault, then roll off your finger the same way you did in Brain Twister and catch it.

Warp Drive

Grab your dilithium crystals and your yo-yo and get ready to boogie out of here. This looks simple, but it's actually quite challenging.

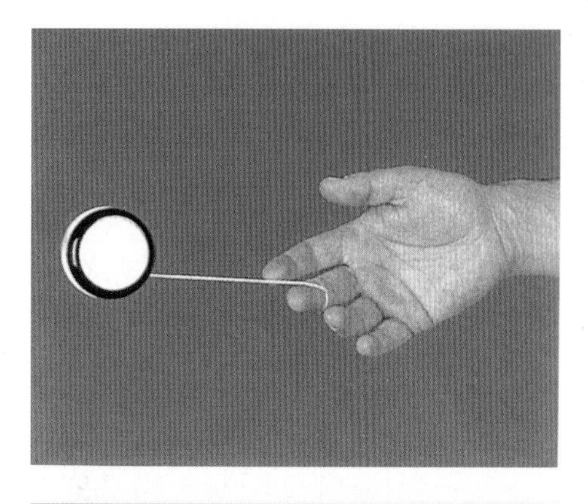

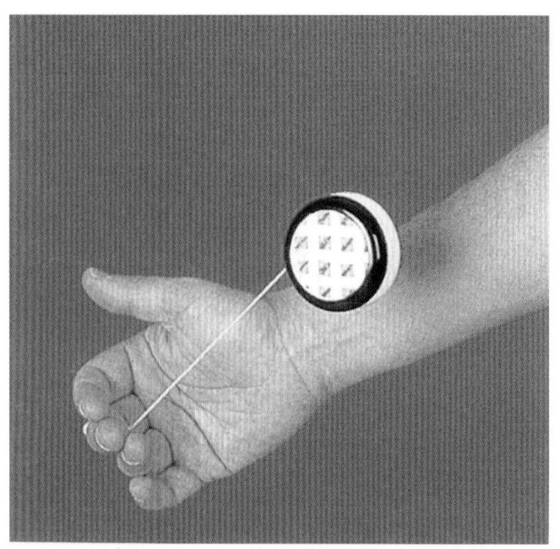

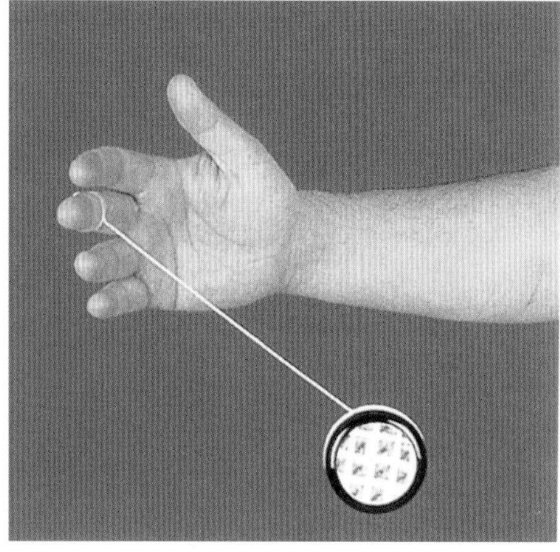

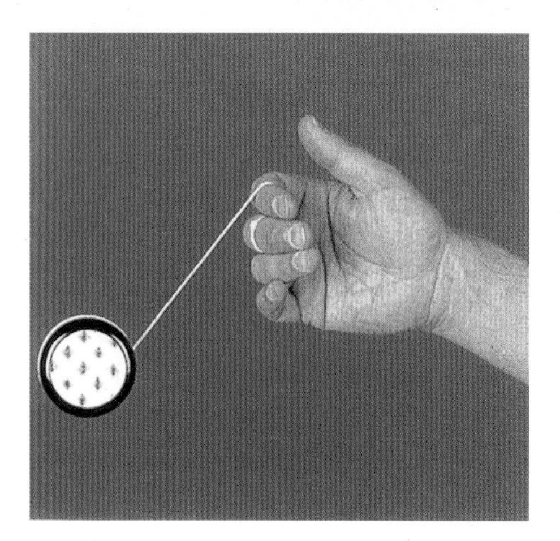

1. Throw a Basic Inside Loop.

2. As it comes back to your hand, give your wrist a hard flick to propel the yo-yo outward into an Around the World.

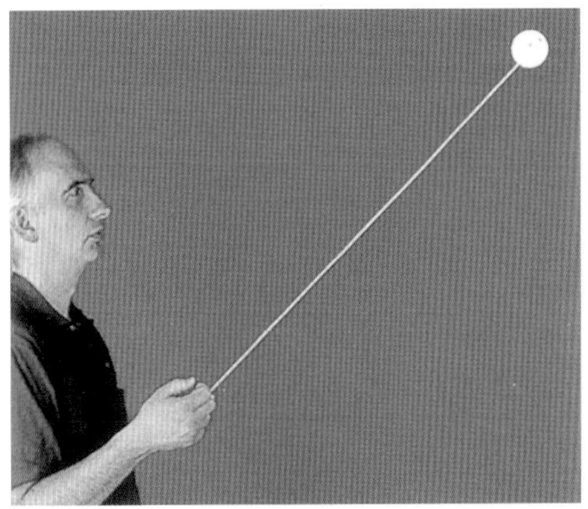

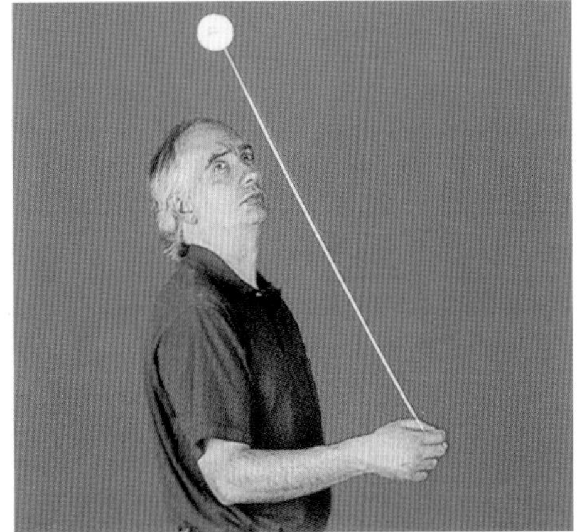

3. Do this again, two more times. Catch the yo-yo after the third Around the World.

Warning: this has the potential to break strings. Make sure you are in a wide-open space with nothing nearby that could be damaged.

Time Warp

☞ ☞ ☞

The tiny silhouetted figure in the bottom right-hand corner of this book is actually part of a yo-yo movie. Flip the pages of the book and you will see the time warp trick!

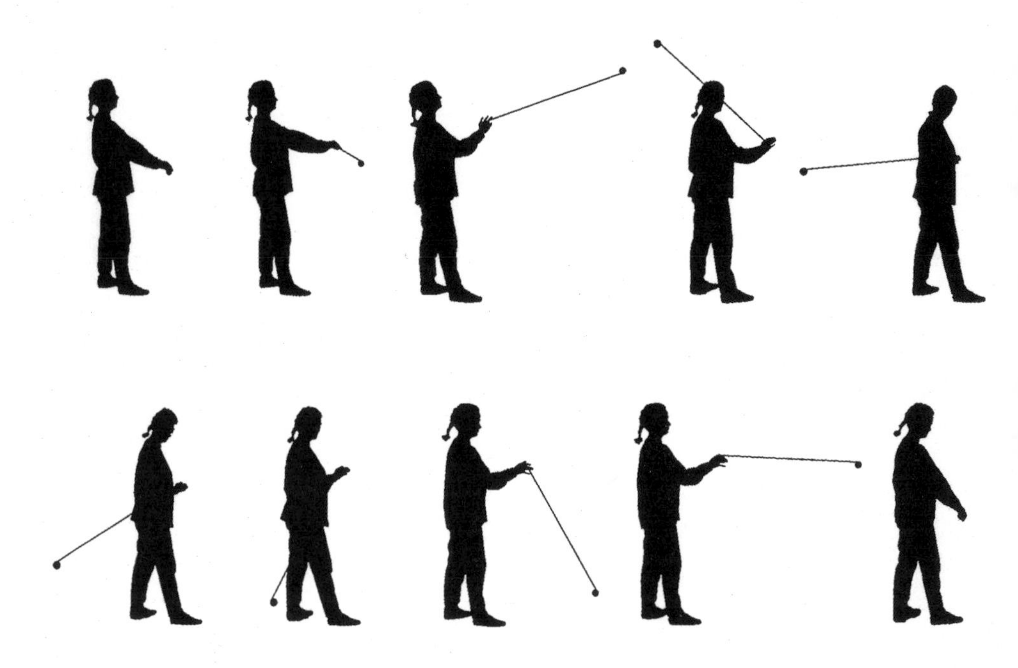

1. Throw a forward Around the World.

2. As it completes its rotation and begins to return to your hand, snap your wrist hard, as in Hop the Fence, which will send the yo-yo into a backward Around the World.

3. As it completes this orbit, bring the yo-yo back to your hand. The fancy term is "regeneration trick."

Two-Handed Tricks

For obvious reasons, you will need two yo-yos for the following tricks. It is recommended that you use two of the same type of yo-yo. Most likely you have only been using your "writing" hand for performing all your tricks. A good way to start is to practice all your basic moves with your other hand. The most important tricks are Hop the Fence and Loops. You'll know you're ready when you can do these without looking at the yo-yo. When you can perform these perfectly, start two-handed yo-yoing.

One expert recommends that you tie your normal yo-yo hand behind you for a week and only practice with your other hand.

Hand behind back

Two-Handed Loops

This one looks really impressive, but will take some time to perfect.

1. Throw a loop with your regular yo-yo hand.

2. As the yo-yo reaches the end of the string, throw the second yo-yo with your other hand. Keep alternating loop throws. The rhythm is an important part of this trick. Relax as you are throwing.

3. Make sure the yo-yo returns are "inside" loops. Practice doing one, then two, then as many as you can without tangling them up.

Two-handed

Milk the Cow

This is an udderly difficult trick to perfect. The trick is to keep the yo-yos moooo-ving.

1. This is simply (and we say that in jest) alternating Hop the Fence. Start by throwing a Hop the Fence with one hand.

2. As the yo-yo gets to the bottom of the string, throw the next yo-yo down.

3. As each yo-yo returns to your hand, flick your wrist to send the yo-yo back down again.

Loops/Reach for the Moon

This doesn't have an official name; this is just how it's referred to in competition.

1. Using one hand, throw a series of Loops.

2. With the other yo-yo hand (usually your stronger or regular hand), throw a series of Reach for the Moon.

3. The trick to performing this is to be able to do the loops without looking because you need to keep an eye on the hand doing Reach the Moon. If you miss a Loop, it's no big deal. If you miss a Reach for the Moon, you can really hit yourself on the head—usually in the mouth.

Ride the Horse

Meanwhile, back at the ranch, the two-handed yo-yo kid was ready to get on a pony.

1. Start by performing Inside Loops with your non-yo-yo hand.

2. With your yo-yo hand, throw repetitions of Hop the Fence. Make sure your hops are situated behind your leg, not in front. These motions together resemble a person riding a horse, hence the name.

Criss Cross

☞☞☞☞

Not a sewing stitch, but a really hard yo-yo maneuver. To give you an idea where your hands should be, hold the yo-yos and cross your hands at the wrists. While you won't be doing this with the yo-yos moving, it gives you an idea of the angle of the yo-yos when they cross each other.

1. Begin by throwing two-handed Loop the Loops.

2. Once you have these moving along cleanly, begin to angle your throws.

3. After several reps, your yo-yos should start to cross each other's paths. Remember when one yo-yo is coming the other is going. This means the yo-yos won't collide in midair. Be prepared for some mishaps while learning this trick.

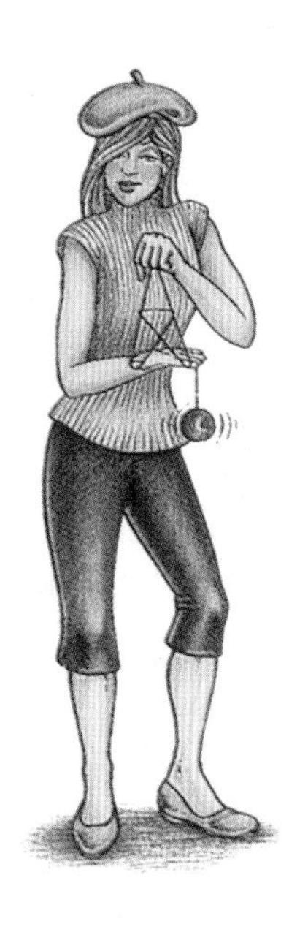

Yo-Yo Pictures

Much like the game of "cat's cradle," use your yo-yo and string to create pictures. Afterward, have your string wind back into your yo-yo.

Eiffel Tower

You don't have to go to Paris to see the Eiffel Tower. You can make one of your own.

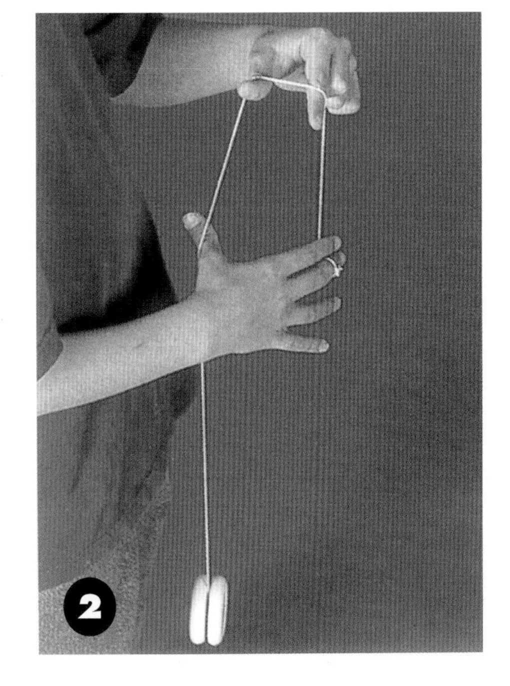

1. Throw a fast or hard Sleeper.

2. Using your free hand, join your index and middle fingers to your thumb.

3. Place the string between your body and free hand.

4. Move your yo-yo hand to move the string over your free hand.

5. As your yo-yo hand comes down, place your thumb against the string. Rotate your hands over each other so the yo-yo hand is on top and the free hand on the bottom.

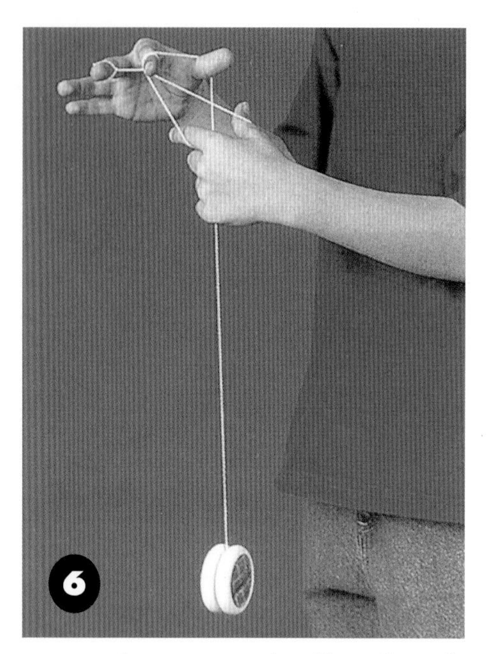

6. You have created a "loop" with your thumb and the fingers of your free hand.

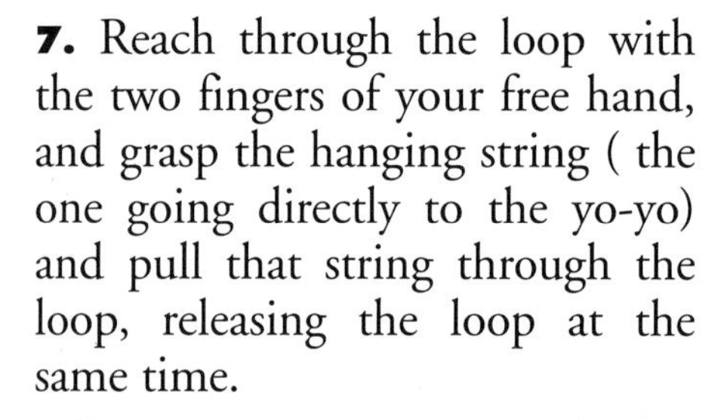

7. Reach through the loop with the two fingers of your free hand, and grasp the hanging string (the one going directly to the yo-yo) and pull that string through the loop, releasing the loop at the same time.

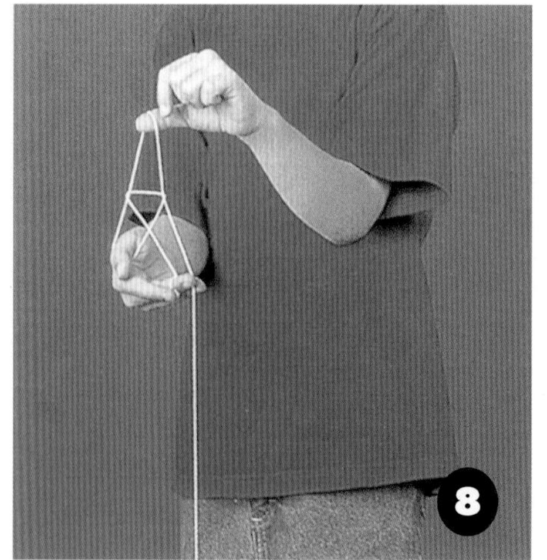

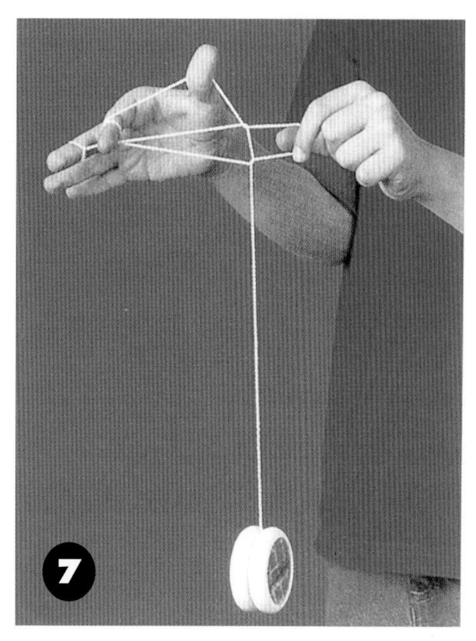

8. Split your hand and fingers to form the "tower."

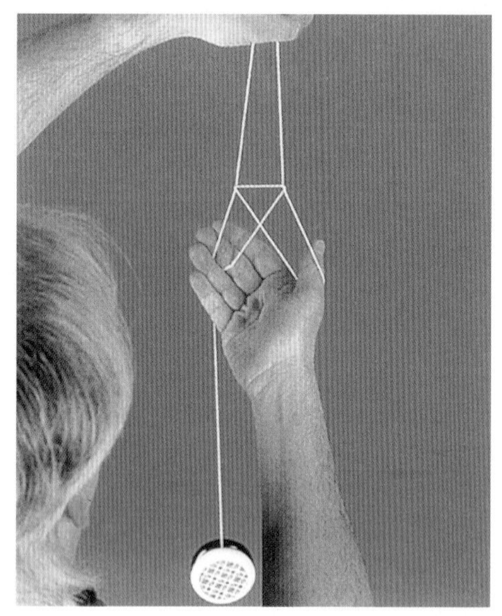

Motorcycle

You don't need a driver's license to do this trick. If you can do the Eiffel Tower, you've got this trick made.

1.. Make the Eiffel Tower. (See above)

2. When you've made the tower, turn it on its side, and "voilà," as they say in France, you have a motorcycle.

3. Allow the yo-yo to spin on the ground, as it does in Walk the Dog, and you now have a moving motorcycle.

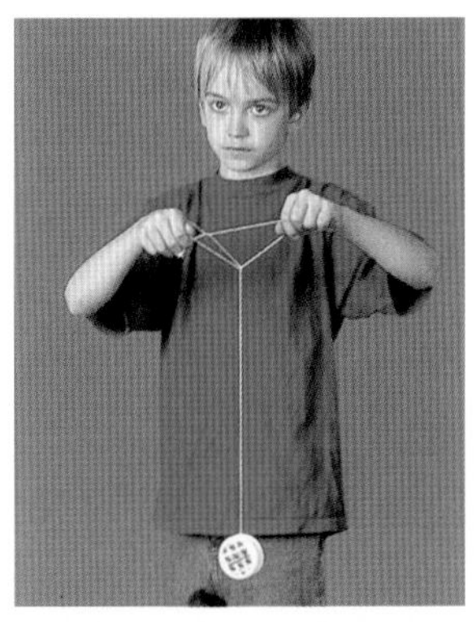

Word "Yo"

Yo Yo Ma is a famous cellist who has not won any yo-yo competitions. But here is a trick you could say was named for him.

1. Make the Eiffel Tower. (See above)

2. Turn your hand over so that the tower is inverted. The yo-yo should be spinning on your left.

3. When viewed head-on, it spells the word "yo."

Index